Human Trafficking, the Bible, and the Church

Human Trafficking, the Bible, and the Church

An Interdisciplinary Study

Marion L. S. Carson

Foreword by Elaine Storkey

scm press

© Marion L. S. Carson, 2016, 2017

First published by Cascade Books
An Imprint of Wipf and Stock Publishers, 2016.
This Edition published in 2017 by SCM Press

Editorial office
Invicta House,
108-114 Golden Lane
London, EC1Y 0TG

Hymns Ancient & Modern® is a registered trademark
of Hymns Ancient and Modern Ltd

SCM Press is an imprint of Hymns Ancient and Modern Ltd (a registered charity)
13a Hellesdon Park Road, Norwich, Norfolk, NR6 5DR

www.scmpress.co.uk

British Library Cataloguing in Publication data

New Revised Standard Version Bible, copyright 1989, Division of Christian Education
of the National Council of the Churches of Christ in the United States of America.
Used by permission. All rights reserved.

A catalogue record for this book is available
from the British Library

978 0 334 05559 4

Printed and bound by
CPI Group (UK) Ltd

In memory of Rev. Dr. Geoffrey Grogan and Mrs. Eva Grogan

Contents

Foreword

Two centuries ago, it took twenty years of activity from the anti-slavery movement in Britain to bring about the ending of the slave trade. And it was fifty years from its formation before it saw the passing of the Abolition of Slavery Act. This time-span seems extraordinary now, when people and governments throughout the whole world agree that slavery is wrong. Yet, all this time later, a movement is, once again, urging us to respond to global injustice. The growing anti-trafficking campaign challenges us to address the iniquity of modern day slavery.

Unlike the early era of slavery, trafficking is not presented as a normal part of a culture's economy. Rarely in public evidence, it is often hidden in the modern globalization of transport and work, for it is not unusual for people to travel vast distances for employment. By its very nature, therefore, trafficking is a crime that often goes unreported, for victims rarely have access to the law, or even to the language of the place to which they are taken. Trafficked victims can be shut away, out of public gaze, or even presented simply as migrant workers. Yet the underlying exploitation, manipulation, denial of freedom and choice remain the same. Now, a complex global structure of organized crime turns people into commodities, where their very bodies are appropriated for the use of others.

At one level, it is not difficult for Christians to respond to this appalling industry. Clearly, it is wrong. It is an abuse of power. It is linked to poverty and deprivation. It forces people against their will to work for others. It manifests a ruthless betrayal of the some of the world's most vulnerable citizens. Yet the deeper issues are more complex. The largest proportion of trafficking is of women and girls into different forms of sex labor. This sits alongside the demand for prostitution evident in cultures across the globe, and it requires us to reflect on our attitudes towards gender and sexuality. It challenges too the assumptions we can easily adopt—which vary from labeling all those women as victims, or creating a false dichotomy between those who deserve justice, and those who operate through "choice." Mindsets are important, because they can obliterate truth and affect our outlook and attitudes towards legislation.

This book is a vital tool in helping Christians to think through these issues, and offers some key theological insights. Most importantly, its focus is overtly biblical, recognizing the importance of the Bible in shaping our values, our framework of understanding, and how we see justice. The study is thorough and scholarly; the author is far more equipped than most of us to work through the complex nature of biblical interpretation and hermeneutics, and she does this with skill. The outcome is earthy and practical, as it moves us to ask important questions of how we should act and respond to this crucial problem in today's world.

Many theological books refine and develop areas that have been studied for decades, if not centuries. Yet Marion Carson cuts new ground. She takes an area outside the normal biblical curriculum, and offers a penetrating analysis of vital key questions. She reflects on history—showing how the different assumptions that Christians brought to the earlier issues of slavery were tied up with unexamined principles of biblical interpretation. She studies the "hermeneutical gap" between pro-slavery advocates, who found legal endorsement of slavery in the Bible and so maintained it was ordained by God, and anti-slavery campaigners, who focused on biblical narratives of redemption and agape love to express God's love for people and hatred of injustice. She treats us to a fascinating study of prostitution in the Bible, including offering various ways for understanding the "whore metaphors." The result is a highly readable book that will refresh our own understanding and help shape our responsibility to bring about change.

What shines through for me is the author's own commitment. Her faithfulness as a believer is reflected in her faithfulness in presenting both the Bible and her interpretative framework. It is also reflected in the underlying pursuit of hope and redemption. Sin need not have the last word. But if slavery is to be defeated and justice triumph, Christians need to allow the Spirit of God to challenge our minds, raise our voices, and direct our actions. This book helps us on that journey.

Elaine Storkey
June 2015

Preface

There is, at present, considerable confusion with regard to the Bible and its place within the life of the church. Some ignore the Scriptures altogether, while others claim that its principles and precepts inform every moment of their lives. Some say that they do not know, and will never know, what its documents might mean, while others are convinced that they do know and will brook no disagreement with their interpretation. There are, of course, many gradations between the two extremes. This state of affairs results not only in divisions within the church, but in the routine side-lining of Scripture in discussions regarding Christian practice.

The difficulties inherent in biblical interpretation for today's world are highlighted when we ask what Scripture might have to say about human trafficking. Over many years' involvement in Christian anti-trafficking work, I have realized that there is a need to help Christians to bridge the hermeneutical gap between the worlds of the Old and New Testaments and our own. To put it bluntly, simplistic readings of Scripture are hindering a Christian response to human trafficking. Some churches refuse to talk about the subject, considering it too shameful to speak of. It is not uncommon for women who have been trafficked into prostitution to be shunned and punished by their churches on the grounds that they are unclean whores (citing, for example, Ezekiel 34 or Revelation 18). Female victims of trafficking are frequently blamed for their situation on the grounds that women are always responsible for the sins of men and that somehow it must have been their fault. Many Christians have reported to me that they have been actively prevented from becoming involved in anti-trafficking work, their church leadership having told them that they should not associate with sinners or that they should be focusing on their own communities.

It is even still possible, on occasion, to hear the view expressed that slavery is in line with God's will, because the Bible says so.

Part of the difficulty is, of course, that biblical hermeneutics is a complex and difficult exercise. We crave simplicity and directness, but, if we are conscientious in trying to avoid selectivity or naiveté in our reading, this can prove elusive. For precisely this reason, speakers, writers, and practitioners often find it easier to base their deliberations on sociology, psychology, and even politics, without reference to the book we claim to be normative for our faith. Disciplines such as these have much to teach us, but if we believe that Scripture has something to say to the church then we must engage with it and try to hear its voice in our time. This book, I hope, will go some way to opening up the question and at the same time, provide a stimulus to theologically informed discussion as to how the church might respond to the tragedy that is contemporary slavery.

Many people have helped me with the production of this book. Anna Forrest, Gudrun Porter, Susan Kershaw, Jonathan Ensor, Professor Noel Peacock and Dr. Ian Shaw provided materials or information. Dr. Philip Ziegler and Professor John Morrison were instrumental in enabling me to work in Trinity College Library, Dublin, where the bulk of the writing was done. Several have read parts of the manuscript at various stages: Professor Murray Pittock, Dr. Anne Pittock, Dr. Martin Spence and Molly Spence, Rev. Dr. Derek Murray, Dr. David Reimer, Rev. Eryl Rowlands. Dr. Derek Newton read through the final manuscript and Rev. Dr. Stephen Chester read my work at various stages in its development, providing valuable insights. Errors and gaps are, needless to say, my responsibility. I am grateful to Dr. John Jeacocke who has used his considerable gifts and eye for detail to correct the final manuscript for publishing, including compiling the indices. The book is dedicated to the memory of my close friends and mentors, Rev. Dr. Geoff and Mrs. Eva Grogan.

Abbreviations

CBQ	*Catholic Biblical Quarterly*
ExpTim	*Expository Times*
HTR	*Harvard Theological Review*
JBR	*Journal of Bible and Religion*
JETS	*Journal of the Evangelical Theological Society*
JJS	*Journal of Jewish Studies*
JSNT	*Journal for the Study of the New Testament*
JSNTSup	Journal for the Study of the New Testament: Supplement Series
JSOT	*Journal for the Study of the Old Testament*
JSOTSup	Journal for the Study of the Old Testament: Supplement Series
NovT	*Novum Testamentum*
NTS	*New Testament Studies*
VT	*Vetus Testamentum*
VTSup	Vetus Testamentum Supplements
ZAW	*Zeitschrift für die alttestamentliche Wissenschaft*

CHAPTER 1

Introduction

1. HUMAN TRAFFICKING: FORMULATING A CHRISTIAN RESPONSE

In the 1800s the transatlantic slave trade was abolished, and today, the prohibition of slavery has "attained *jus cogens* status."[1] In other words, it has been recognized as illegal in international law. Nevertheless, millions of people are enslaved throughout the world. From a Christian perspective it should go without saying that we ought to work towards the eradication of this evil. Surely, the existence of slavery contradicts everything that we understand of God's love for his people? Certainly, many Christians are involved in tackling the problem. At grass roots level they are engaged in rescue, rehabilitation, and prevention work. At the political level, they are involved in lobbying, campaigning, and policy making.

In order to do this work effectively, however, it is crucial that Christians are able to respond to the issues in an informed manner. Much has been written on the sociological, economic, and political aspects of modern-day slavery as well as the psychology of its effects on victims, and it is right that we wrestle with complex issues such as poverty, criminality, globalization, and migration—all of which have a direct bearing on human trafficking.[2]

---

1 Bassiouni, "Enslavement," 445.

2. On the causes of human trafficking, see Shelley, *Human Trafficking*, 37–58.

1

We also need, however, to think through the theological foundations of the enterprise, and since all Christian traditions still consider the Bible to be normative for faith and practice, it is appropriate that we start there.[3] Views of the extent to which the biblical literature should inform Christian living vary from tradition to tradition, but all are agreed that as the earliest evidence of God's self-revelation in Christ, the Bible provides the basis for theological reflection and ethical response to God's work in his creation. Not only that, it is believed that God continually speaks through Scripture. In the words of John Webster, Scripture's role is "God's self-communication, that is the acts of Father, Son, and Spirit which establish and maintain that saving fellowship with humankind in which God makes himself known to us and by us."[4]

In the light of this shared understanding of Scripture, the purpose of this book is to ask what the Bible has to say about contemporary human trafficking. In order to answer this, I propose to ask two questions. First, what does the Bible say about slavery in general? How can it inform a Christian response to modern-day trafficking of persons? Second, it is my intention to consider a particular subset of modern-day slavery—sex trafficking. While many slaves find that they are subject to sexual exploitation and abuse, the sheer numbers of women and children who are trafficked into the sex trade to work in prostitution suggests that the current situation is unlike anything that has gone on before. How should Christians respond to this, and how can the Bible help them to do so?

2. SETTING THE HERMENEUTICAL SCENE

Our main method of exploring these questions will be to conduct a survey of major biblical passages dealing with slavery and prostitution. However, it is important that we recognize the hermeneutical prerequisites for such a task. Any interpretation of Scripture for contemporary application requires us to be aware of the current situation with regard to slavery—we need to know the situation into which we are bringing biblically informed perspectives. Our first task will therefore be to give an outline of human trafficking in its various forms throughout the world today. After this, however, we will have to note two very important hermeneutical questions that are often

3. See Fowl, *Engaging Scripture*, 2; Goldingay, *Models for Scripture*; Schneiders, *The Revelatory Text*; Wright, *Scripture and the Authority of God*.

4. Webster, *Holy Scripture*, 8.

overlooked in discussions of Christian responses to human trafficking—the difference between the situation confronting us today and that reflected in the biblical texts, and the church's rather checkered history with regard to responses to prostitution.

Contemporary Slavery

It is important to distinguish between trafficking and people smuggling.[5] In the latter, individuals pay money to travel illegally from one country to another, usually for the purposes of employment. In other words, they give their consent to the transaction. In human trafficking, no such consent is given, as the definition of the United Nations makes clear. Human trafficking is

> the recruitment, transportation, transfer, harbouring or receipt of persons, by means of the threat or use of force or other forms of coercion, of abduction, of fraud, of deception, of the abuse of power or of a position of vulnerability or of the giving or receiving of payments or benefits to achieve the consent of a person having control over another person, for the purpose of exploitation. Exploitation shall include at a minimum, the exploitation of the prostitution of others or other forms of sexual exploitation, forced labour or services, slavery or practices similar to slavery, servitude or the removal of organs.[6]

The numbers of those considered to have been trafficked is generally considered to be enormous, with some estimates at twenty-seven million.[7] It is, however, impossible to give exact numbers, simply because of the covert nature of human trafficking. In some cases, the lines between trafficking and smuggling become blurred. For example, someone who starts out knowingly and willingly to go into a line of work can quickly find that his or her situation is impossible and that an apparently safe agreement becomes coercive, fraudulent, or violent. Another problem is that one person's view of exploitation and coercion may not be the same as another's. For example, people in abject poverty may be only too grateful to be given the means to survive—even if they are technically enslaved.

5. See Bales, *Understanding Global Slavery*, 132.

6. Article 3, paragraph (a) of The United Nations Protocol to Prevent, Suppress and Punish Trafficking in Persons.

7. So Bales, *Disposable People*, 8.

There are several different forms of human trafficking today. *Chattel slavery*, the "traditional" type of slavery in which one person uses another as his or her property, constitutes the smallest grouping and is a feature of warfare.[8] One famous account of this is in Mende Nazer's autobiography in which she tells of being kidnapped as a child from her village and sold into domestic slavery.[9] In *debt slavery*, which is especially prevalent in India, Pakistan, and South America, families find themselves working in domestic work, mines, agriculture, or brick-making to pay fictitious but enforced debts. However, the work they do is never enough, as the "lender" controls the amount to be repaid, and arbitrary interest rates, as well as medical bills and funeral costs, are added to the initial debt.[10]

In *bonded* or *forced labor*, workers find themselves trapped in exploitative and dangerous conditions. Without pension or health insurance, they work in construction sites, mines, and charcoal producing camps, unable to leave. Migrant workers are particularly at risk from criminal organizations. Many are tricked into believing that emigration will lead to an improvement in their circumstances, or those of their families, only to find that they are forced to work for little or no pay. Although bonded and forced labor is illegal in most countries, the perpetrators are seldom caught and punished.

In *sex slavery*, women and children and some men are forced to work as prostitutes.[11] Kidnapping women and girls for sexual use by soldiers is particularly prevalent in unstable societies and in wartime. The most famous example of this is the use of Japanese "comfort women" by the Korean army in the 1930s and 1940s.[12] More recently kidnap for the purposes of sexual exploitation has been a feature of Islamicizing jihad in Africa and the Middle East. In East Asia, girls are sold by impoverished rural families to work in city brothels. Throughout south-east Asia there is a huge market in young girls, because virginity commands a larger price. Many girls from Eastern Europe find themselves in a form of debt bondage to gang members who trick them into working as prostitutes. Huge sums of money

8. On the various forms of contemporary slavery see the *Trafficking in Persons Report* which is produced yearly by the United States State Department; Weissbrodt, *Abolishing Slavery*; Shelley, *Human Trafficking*; Bales, *Disposable People*. The groupings described here are not necessarily separate.

9. Nazer, *Slave*.

10. Bales, *Understanding Global Slavery*, 2.

11. On sex trafficking see Kara, *Sex Trafficking*; Malarek, *The Natashas*. See further the accounts in Ivison, *Fiona's Story* and Forsyth, *Slave Girl*.

12. Soh, *Comfort Women*.

are to be made by those who provide the women and girls to work in bars, clubs, private apartments, or on urban streets. For, as Siddharth Kara notes, prostitution is relatively cheap to run:

> Drug trafficking generates greater dollar revenues, but trafficked women are far more profitable. Unlike a drug, a human female does not have to be grown, cultivated, distilled or packaged. Unlike a drug, a human female can be used by the customer again and again.[13]

A further category is *child labor*. In Uganda and Burma (among others), children are abducted from their families and trained as soldiers. Threatened with torture if they try to escape, they are taught to use weapons. The mortality rate is high and the psychological damage done to the children inestimable. In the Philippines too, children as young as five years old work on farms and plantations, in factories and bakeries. In the Caribbean, children can be kept as domestic servants (known as *restavecs*) until adulthood.[14] Lastly, in *activities akin to slavery*, women are sold as brides over the internet, children are groomed and tricked into providing sexual services to criminal gangs, and individuals are forced into selling their organs, or those of their children, for transplant purposes. Recognition of these new forms of slavery, by organizations such as Anti-Slavery International, leads to the conclusion that there are more slaves in the world today than when the British parliament passed the antislavery act of 1807.

The Bible and Slavery: The Hermeneutical Gap

The philosophical battle against slavery has been won.[15] We have come a long way from Aristotle's idea that human beings fall into two categories, the natural master and the natural slave.[16] The dictum of the Universal Declaration of Human Rights that "No one shall be held in slavery or servitude; slavery and the slave trade shall be prohibited in all their forms" is hardly up for debate.[17] As Kevin Bales says,

13. Kara, *Sex Trafficking*, x.

14. Cadet, *Restavec*. Other personal accounts of slavery include Bok, *Escape from Slavery*; Gupta, *Enslaved*.

15. See, however, the discussion of a newspaper report in the *New York Times* on 10th May 1996 by Glancy in "House Reading and Field Readings."

16. Politics 1254b28–34. See Garnsey, *Ideas of Slavery*, 108–10.

17. *Article 4, Universal Declaration of Human Rights.*

> We do not have to win the moral argument against slavery; no
> government or organized interest group is pressing the case that
> slavery is desirable or even acceptable. No priest or minister is
> standing in the pulpit and giving biblical justifications for slavery.
> No philosophers offer up rationalisations for slavery.[18]

Christians may no longer be giving biblical justifications for slavery, but many do still look to the Bible to inform their daily lives and guide them, and this raises profound questions for any discussion of human trafficking. For, throughout the biblical literature, slavery is accepted as the norm, and nowhere is there a direct prohibition against it. So what should we do? We could remove the Bible completely. Hector Avalos argues, for example, that the Bible is pro-slavery and is "one of the greatest obstacles to human ethical progress in history" and should be jettisoned altogether as being without moral authority.[19] However, from a Christian point of view this would be to deny the foundations of the church's ethical thinking—hardly a truthful approach. Thus, we have to ask, can the Bible, whose teaching on slavery is so at odds with our contemporary worldview, inform efforts to end human trafficking, and if so, how?

Fortunately, Christians who believe that the Bible should have a place in the conversation can look to historical precedent for help. The end of the Atlantic slave trade came about, to a large extent, because Christians campaigned against it. These Christians considered the slave trade to be contrary to the will of God, but they also loved their Scriptures. It will be of great help to consider the part the Bible played in their deliberations and how they reconciled their hostility to slavery with their belief that the Bible was a source for their work. Thus, in chapter 2 we will look at the history of the abolitionist campaign and the role of the Bible in it. What lessons can be learned from the approach of the abolitionists to Scripture which might help Christians today? I shall suggest that although the place of the Bible in the antislavery campaign was different on either side of the Atlantic, social change was facilitated by means of an intuitive hermeneutic that found stimulus and support in the narrative of redemption, while a more literal approach, which looked to the Bible for direct prescription, proved ineffectual and indeed hindered the challenging of injustice.

18. Kevin Bales, "How We Will End Slavery," 29–30.

19. Avalos, *Slavery, Abolitionism and the Ethics of Biblical Studies,* 288. Avalos writes from the perspective of New Atheism.

Having done this we will then proceed, in chapter 3, to consider the biblical material itself. Many advances have been made in biblical scholarship since the time of the abolitionists. How does their hermeneutical approach stand up in the light of these scholarly findings? We will conduct a survey of key texts that deal with slavery, not only with a view to determining how they might have been understood in their original contexts, but also to discern how, if at all, they might apply in a Christian response to slavery in its contemporary forms. We shall see that the instinct of the abolitionists with regard to reading the Bible in the face of human suffering and injustice provides us with a hermeneutic for biblically informed anti-slavery work today.

Christians and the Sex Trade

The majority of people in slavery today are caught up in bonded labor or debt slavery. However, a large component of contemporary human trafficking involves the sale of women and children into the sex industry to work as prostitutes, and unfortunately, consciously or unconsciously, this can so color public responses as to hinder not only balanced discussion of how to tackle it, but also compassionate response to the victims. The shame associated with prostitution can lead to extreme reactions. For example, O'Connor and Healy report that in Albania, a woman who has been involved in prostitution will be deemed to have dishonored her family and is at risk of being killed by them—even if she was trafficked.[20] In fact, prostitutes themselves are held in such disdain by many (if not most) societies that they are often considered to be unworthy of help, and this stigma applies whether they have been victims of human trafficking or not. Often it is implicitly suggested that they are to blame for their situation, fostering an attitude of indifference. In Gilbert King's experience, for example, once the media defines the victims of traffickers as "prostitutes,"

> in one quick breath, empathy, outrage, and the most basic human rights are obliterated. The world is simply unmoved by more stories of Russian "prostitutes" with pimp problems in the Balkans, or young Thai girls with HIV having unprotected sex in massage parlors in Bangkok, let alone New York or Chicago.[21]

20. O'Connor and Healy, *The Links between Prostitution and Sex Trafficking*, 9.
21. King, *Woman, Child for Sale*, 7–8.

For the church's part, attitudes to prostitution and prostitutes have tended to be rather polarized. Historically, prostitutes have been seen either as sinners *par excellence*, requiring to be punished or reformed, or as the recipients of special grace, particularly close to God. Today, in many if not most churches, the subject of prostitution is rarely discussed, and even avoided as taboo. This must raise the question: how far are our views of those involved in prostitution culturally conditioned and how far are they theologically informed? There is a need for Christians to be aware of their own preconceptions and prejudices, and to be open to allowing these to be challenged and transformed by the biblical texts.

There is another reason why this question must be addressed. Attitudes to prostitution directly affect the discussion of how sex trafficking should be tackled. There is today a very influential argument which suggests that if prostitution were to be decriminalized, and considered a job like any other, the illicit sex industry would disappear and the trafficking of women and children reduce. What should a Christian response be to this question? Should it be dismissed out of hand as condoning sin, or considered as a way to reduce suffering?

Other factors need to be considered. Various cultural differences affect how sex-trafficking is viewed throughout the world. In the poorest groupings in India (for example), prostitution may be the only option available for some women, while selling girls into the sex trade might be the only way of survival for near destitute families. Should these families be deprived of their only means of survival? Moreover, in Thailand or Japan visits to brothels are considered culturally acceptable, a legitimate form of entertainment which is no different from going to the opera or museum. To what extent should these views be respected?

The second half of this book is intended to help readers think these complex and emotive questions through. In chapter 4, we will consider attitudes to prostitution throughout history. My first aim will be to point out and explore the ambivalence and double standards that often pertain to discussions of prostitution and I will do so by means of a literary portrait of attitudes to prostitution, namely, Guy de Maupassant's short story *Boule de Suif*. We will then introduce and explore various moral arguments, the current debate as to whether or not prostitution is intrinsically exploitative, and the relationship of this debate to questions of anti-trafficking policy. The overall aim of the chapter is not so much to provide an answer to the questions raised as to expose their complexity and discourage simplistic, ill-informed and emotively based responses. I hope to enable readers to recognize their hermeneutical presuppositions and contexts in preparation for approaching the biblical texts.

Acknowledging once again the normative role of Scripture in Christian thinking, in chapter 5 we will return to the biblical literature to consider whether it can help us to determine what (if anything) is wrong with prostitution and what a Christian response to the sex trade might be. Building on the hermeneutical approach explored in chapter 3, our strategy will again be to look at key passages in which prostitution is directly mentioned. To what extent can the biblical texts inform discussions of contemporary sex trafficking and contribute to a Christian response? In the concluding chapter, we will draw the results of our enquiry together, offering observations and suggestions as to the place of the Bible in discussion of human trafficking as a whole.

3. A NOTE ON METHODOLOGY

In the course of the study we will draw on several disciplines. In order to investigate how the Bible was understood during the abolitionist campaign we will give an historical account of the anti-slavery campaign in Britain and America, looking at the way the Bible was read at that time, and the cultural influences on its interpreters—intellectuals, slaveholders, clergy, and the slaves themselves. As we consider the rights and wrongs of the sex trade we will draw on history, literature, and philosophical discussions of the topic, as well as feminist and sociological studies of contemporary prostitution and human trafficking.

When we come to look at the biblical texts themselves, we will make use of some of the developments in biblical studies that have taken place since the time of the abolitionists. In order to ground the texts in their own time, the historical-critical method will be our first port of call. We will also draw on various methods that have developed from the historical-critical approach, including rhetorical and narrative criticism. In particular, social-scientific approaches will help us to understand more of how the worlds represented by the texts might have functioned, and to see them as "vehicles for social acts"—in other words, to see the kind of socioeconomic and psychological forces at work in the lives of the people reflected in them.[22] Thus, our focus is on *how* the texts might have worked, rather than

---

22. Brueggemann, *The Book that Breathes New Life*, 101. On social-scientific criticism

on the questions of fact that preoccupied the first generations of historical critics. When we come to consider prostitution in the Bible, we will draw extensively on feminist readings, not because of any particular agenda, but because very often it is feminist writers, more than any others, who have tackled the texts under consideration and shed new light on them. As David Pleins writes,

> Social-scientific, feminist, and liberation readings assist in the re-construction of the plausible sociopolitical matrices for the biblical materials by taking up the challenge of a historical and critical exegesis while exposing the ideological underpinnings of the text through revised reconstructions of the text's social moorings and transmission. By this type of analysis we can enter the social world of the biblical authors. We can begin to see the contexts of the struggles of women, day laborers, and the poor in ancient Israel. The recovery of these ancient marginalized voices has enabled us to more fully appreciate the depth and scope of the biblical debates over justice in society.[23]

With the help of these approaches, then, we will be able to consider how these ancient texts can speak to the questions that are exercising us in this study. There is, however, another problem. The Bible contains so many documents of differing genres, times, and even worldviews, that it may be doubted that it can be of any use in ethical discussion at all.[24] Nevertheless, it is the belief of the Christian church that, for all its diversity, there is a coherence in the collection of documents that it calls the Bible. In this view, the biblical writers are all articulating, in a variety of ways, the relationship between humanity and God in history. The Hebrew Scriptures (or what Christians refer to as the Old Testament) are to be understood in the light of the person and work of Jesus Christ, the Messiah of Jewish expectation. It is with this in mind that we will adopt a canonical approach to the biblical literature, one that considers the documents taken together and in the form in which we have them today.[25] This kind of approach, most famously promulgated by Brevard Childs, is particularly useful for the development

see Elliott, *What is Social Scientific Criticism?*

23. Pleins, *The Social Visions of the Hebrew Bible*, 22–23.

24. On the problems of using the Bible for ethical instruction see Bartholomew, "How Has the Bible Been Used Ethically?"

25. Birch & Rasmussen, *Bible and Ethics in the Christian Life*. See further J. L. H. McDonald, *Biblical Interpretation and Christian Ethics*. On the development of the canon see L. M. McDonald, *The Biblical Canon*.

of a biblical view on ethical questions. For in the canon we can see how the people of Yahweh (Old Testament) and followers of Jesus Christ (New Testament) attempted to respond to the divine, whom they understood to make ethical demands.[26] Since Christians also believe that God continues to speak through these Scriptures, the church's task is to try to interpret them in order to hear what the divine call might be in the present day. As Robert Wall says,

> The act of reinterpreting Scripture as the vehicle of God's truth and grace, however provisional and seemingly tentative, is the courageous act of finding God's intended meaning for a community of faith who in faith seeks after a more mature life with Christ in the realm of his Spirit.[27]

Admittedly, the task is not without its difficulties.[28] First, the very notion of a canon of Scripture is problematic, for there are varying ideas amongst the traditions as to which books constitute the canon. For example, the Roman Catholic and Greek Orthodox churches have more Old Testament books in their canon than the Protestant denominations do.[29] Second, the material contained in the canon is so extensive that it is very difficult for any one study to do it justice. Both slavery and prostitution receive extensive attention in the Bible—for example, in the legal material, narratives, epistles, and metaphorically. Any investigation of these subjects in Scripture must entail judicious decisions as to how much material will be considered. Third, there is a danger of losing sight of the diversity within the canon, not to mention the centuries of scholarship that have attempted to understand its documents. By viewing the books together, we run the

26. Childs, *Biblical Theology*. The main critic of Childs' approach is James Barr. See his *The Concept of Biblical Theology*, 401–38. The canonical approach is followed by Birch, *Let Justice Roll Down*.

27. Wall, "The Significance of a Canonical Perspective," 531. See further, Brueggemann, *The Book that Breathes New Life*, 25: "The Bible is not a fixed, frozen readily exhausted read; it is rather a 'script' always reread, through which the Spirit makes new."

28. See the discussion in Davies, *Immoral Bible*, 63–100. For critique of Childs see Brett, *Biblical Criticism in Crisis? See* further Noble, *The Canonical Approach*.

29. Roman Catholics accept Tobit, Judith, Wisdom, Ben Sira, 1 and 2 Maccabees and some additions to Jeremiah, Esther, and Daniel in the Hebrew canon. The Greek Orthodox church, which recognizes the Septuagint rather than the Masoretic text, also has the "Apocrypha," but has in addition 1 and 2 Esdras, the Prayer of Manasseh, Psalm 151, 3 Maccabees, Odes of Solomon, 4 Maccabees. See Goldingay, *Approaches to Old Testament Interpretation*, 138–45. See further Barton, *People of the Book?* 24–35; Lienhard, *The Bible, the Church, and Authority*.

risk of disregarding the vast timescale represented, and ignoring the contradictions and tensions. In other words, there is a danger of oversimplifying a very complex book.

For all these reasons, it is important to establish certain limits to this study. First, with regard to the extent of the canon, I have confined myself to that accepted by the Protestant churches, partly because to extend the enquiry would make it unwieldy, but more importantly, because there is no contention as to the canonicity of these texts amongst all traditions of the church.[30] Second, rather than attempt to cover every mention of or allusion to slavery and prostitution in the canon, I will conduct a survey of key texts directly relating to our subjects of slavery and prostitution. We will be unable to look at passages dealing with closely related ideas, for example, personhood, property, sexuality, or community. Nevertheless, as we shall see, within these parameters, there is enough material for us to attempt to discern a consistent moral view regarding slavery and prostitution in the biblical literature. By taking account of genre and historical context (insofar as this is possible), I hope to be able to do justice to the variety of voices without losing sight of the fact that centuries of human reflection on the relationship between humanity and God are represented in these documents.

Finally, while it is one thing to try to understand the biblical texts in their original settings, it is quite another to be able to get from there to our own world today. In other words, there is the hermeneutical problem of enabling application of these texts to our contemporary situation. It is here that the nineteenth-century abolitionists can help us. As I have suggested, many committed Christians were able to hold together a hatred of slavery and a love of the Scriptures in creative tension. They were able to effect radical social change, believing that their activities were entirely in tune with the teachings of their faith. How did they do this? What hermeneutical approach to Scripture enabled them to take this view? It is the task of our next chapter to find out.

---

30. There is difference of opinion regarding the version—whether the Hebrew or the LXX Greek translation of the Hebrew Bible—to be used. Here I will use the MT.

CHAPTER 2

The Bible
and the
Abolitionist Debate

1. INTRODUCTION

Christians today are universally agreed that slavery is unacceptable. Given that this is the case, it seems extraordinary that there could ever have been debate regarding its moral legitimacy within the church. Yet it was so. Slavery was considered normative by most Christians until well into the 1700s and change came about only after a long, hard struggle. The place of the Bible in that struggle is well known. Protagonists on both sides of the debate found authority for their stance in the Scriptures. But ultimately the battle yielded an about-turn in the received idea of what the Bible had to say about slavery. At the beginning, most Christians believed that the Bible permitted slavery. At the end, the universal view was that it demanded that the practice be stopped on the basis of the "law of love."[1]

This chapter explores how this change came about. In order to do so I will ask two questions. First, I will consider the part that Scripture played in the abolitionist debate. How did the campaigners on both sides use the

---

1. See Meeks, "The 'Haustafeln' and American Slavery."

Bible, and what impact did that use have on the course of the campaign? Second, I will examine the hermeneutical presuppositions and approaches that informed their use of the Bible. What intellectual, cultural, and social influences enabled the change to take place? As we shall see, the course of the antislavery debate, and the role of the Bible in it, took very different forms in Britain and America.

2. QUAKER ANTI-SLAVERY THINKING IN AMERICA AND BRITAIN

In the American colonies, change began in the 1670s, when some Quakers questioned the compatibility of slave-holding with their principles of equality and non-violence.[2] However, because slaveholding was economically profitable, the idea was slow to take hold. It was not until 1758 that the Philadelphia Yearly Meeting decided that slaveholders should be disowned, when disapproving reports in Europe that American Quakers "do here handel men as they handel there cattle" shamed them into action.[3]

The writings of John Woolman and Anthony Benezet took antislavery ideas beyond Quakerism.[4] Gradually, the northern states changed their legislation, banning the further import of slaves. However, as numbers of slaves in the North reduced, so they increased in the plantations of the South, particularly after 1793 when the invention of the cotton gin ensured that the demand for cotton could be more speedily met. In 1808, the importation of slaves was banned throughout the United States. Increasingly contentious, slavery became central to the discussion of which territories should be admitted to the Union. In 1850, The Fugitive Slave Law decreed that runaways to the Northern free States could be returned to their Southern owners. However, when many in the North refused to comply, Southern states objected to the infringement of their rights. War ensued. After the North's victory, the Emancipation Declaration signed by President Lincoln came into effect on January 1st, 1863. Slavery ended, in

2. Enslavement was commonly a consequence of war, and violence was necessary to maintain the system. See Brown, *Moral Capital,* 88. For an introduction to Quaker history and ideas, see Durham, *Spirit of the Quakers.*

3. See Soderlund, *Quakers and Slavery,* 177 for the view that American Quakers were motivated not so much by revulsion against slaveholding but the desire to maintain the purity of their Society.

4. Davis, *Problem of Slavery in Western Culture,* 319–62; Frost, *Quaker Origins of Antislavery.*

theory, in 1865 when the 13th Amendment to the Constitution banned it altogether.[5]

In Britain, too, anti-slavery thinking began among the Quakers, its growth fertilized by transatlantic travel and the works of Benezet and Woolman. In 1783, a Quaker committee presented a petition containing 273 signatures to the House of Commons, objecting to the traffic of slaves. Four years later Thomas Clarkson and Granville Sharp, both tireless anti-slavery campaigners, joined with the Quakers to form the non-denominational Society for Effecting the Abolition of the Slave Trade.

The campaign gained momentum. The work of William Wilberforce and the evangelical "Clapham sect" was crucial for the political struggle and attitudinal change in the country as a whole.[6] After a lull when revolution in France frightened many into thinking that abolitionists were "Jacobins," the Slave Trade Act was passed in 1807. Parliament's reluctance to legislate for complete abolition finally gave way in 1833 when the Slavery Abolition Act became law, the campaign having been led by another evangelical, Thomas Fowell Buxton.

3. ANTI-SLAVERY AND THE BIBLE

From the beginning, Quakers objected to slavery on the basis of the "Golden Rule". As early as 1688, in the first recorded written protest against slavery in North America, the Germantown Pennsylvania congregation of Mennonite Quakers wrote to their monthly meeting: "There is a saying, that we should do to all men like as we will be done ourselves; making no difference of what generation, descent or colour they are."[7]

The appeal to the Golden Rule, and indeed to the Bible as a whole, became a major feature of the Quaker campaign. Benezet's influential pamphlet of 1760, *Observations on the Inslaving, Importing and Purchasing of Negroes*, began with a reminder of the command to love God and one another. Slavery, with all its concomitant suffering, was, he wrote, inconsistent with the gospel. His 1785 work, *A Caution to Great Britain*, emphasized equality between white and black people, calling the latter "our fellow-creatures, as free as ourselves by nature." Like Israel, which experienced famine

5. For the main events in America, see Kolchin, *American Slavery*; Morgan, *Slavery in America*; Fogel, *Without Consent or Contract*.

6. See Howse, *Saints in Politics*; Tomkins, *The Clapham Sect*.

7. Reprinted in Morgan, *Slavery in America*, 370.

following the treatment of the Gibeonites (2 Sam 21:1), England would feel the wrath of God because of its unjust treatment of the Negroes. The principle of equality, on which the Quaker movement had been founded, had been flouted: "God gave to man dominion over the fish of the sea, and over the fowls of the air, and over the cattle &c. but imposed no involuntary subjection of one man to another."[8] No race could be said to be inferior on the grounds of the sins of their fathers, or be precluded from the possibility of salvation.[9]

In 1783, the London Yearly Meeting of the Quakers issued a "publick testimony" against the slave trade. The suffering inflicted by slave-owners was neither Christian nor befitting of Englishmen. Once again they turned to the Bible to support their cause. Quoting Jeremiah 22:13, they warned that God, the righteous judge, would chastise nations for their sins: "Woe unto him, that buildeth his house by unrighteousness, and his chambers by wrong; that useth his neighbour's service without wages and giveth him not for his work."[10] Clearly, God would not allow prosperity if the direct contravention of this prophecy was maintained by the legislature.

These new ideas had to be tested, however, and not all agreed with the Quaker stance. In 1772, the British Anglican priest Thomas Thompson declared slavery to be in line with Levitical law, which Jesus did not repeal.[11] Against this, Granville Sharp argued that the Bible also commanded benevolence to strangers, and cited the Parable of the Good Samaritan in support.[12] In 1788, in a work commissioned by Liverpool slave traders, Raymond Harris, a former Jesuit priest, argued for slavery on the grounds that Abraham had slaves: those who opposed slave traders were hostile to the will of God.[13] Rev. James Ramsay responded by pointing to the iniquities that accompanied the Liverpool slave trade, and noting that he would not want his family to be treated in the way that slaves were.[14] In Scotland, similar arguments took place. For example, in response to the point that

---

8. Morgan, *Slavery in America*, 28–29.

9. Frost, *Quaker Origins*, 2.

10. Dilwyn and Lloyd, *The Case of Our Fellow-Creatures*, 15. On Quakers and the slave trade in Britain see Anstey, *Atlantic Slave Trade and British Abolition*, 200–235.

11. Thompson, *The African Trade for Negro Slaves*.

12. Sharp, *The Just Limitation on Slavery*.

13. Harris, "Scriptural Researches on the Licitness of the Slave Trade."

14. Ramsay, *Examination of the Rev Mr Harris's Scriptural Researches*.

Scripture did not forbid slavery, Alan Mcconnochie argued in court in 1776 that it was "inconsistent with the principles and spirit" of Christianity.[15]

As awareness of the sufferings of slaves increased, attitudes began to change. James Ramsay's first-hand accounts of the Caribbean sugar plantations and the "Middle Passage" spurred Granville Sharp and Thomas Clarkson on to campaign throughout Great Britain and beyond.[16] In churches throughout the land, clergy began to warn of dire punishment—the slave trade contravened the justice envisaged by the prophets. Britain would share the fate of Tyre, which had also traded in human beings (Ezek 27:13). Prosperity required a foundation of righteousness, or it would fall (Joel 3:16–21).[17]

John Wesley, in his "Thoughts Upon Slavery" (1774) reminded slave-holders of divine judgment, declaring that on "that day it shall be more tolerable for Sodom and Gomorrah than for you. The blood of thy brother crieth against thee from the earth. Africans are creatures of God, for whom Christ died."[18]

Thus, for those concerned with the alleviation of suffering and injustice, the more empathic approach to Scriptures championed by Quakers and others seemed much more conducive to change than the legalism that wanted to maintain the status quo.[19] The Golden Rule (or "law of love") expressed all that needed to be said.[20] As Granville Sharp wrote, the Golden Rule was the "sum and essence of the whole Law of God."[21]

Despite the fact that the debate on both sides of the Atlantic was led by Christians, the Bible was to play a less prominent part in British abolitionism than in America. While bolstered by biblical themes and motifs, the argument tended to focus on pragmatics and economics—"devout Victorians assumed that good economics was consistent with good religion."[22] The slave trade was, the planters argued, important for the British economy;

15. See Whyte, *Scotland and the Abolition of Black Slavery 1756–1838*, 29.

16. Ramsay, *Essay on the Treatment and Conversion of African Slaves.*

17. See, for example, Agutter, "The Abolition of the Slave Trade considered in a Religious Point of View." See also Briggs, "Baptists and the Campaign to Abolish the Slave Trade."

18. Wesley, *Thoughts upon Slavery*, 52.

19. For the idea of a Quaker "hermeneutic of empathy" see Palmer, "Did William Penn Diverge Significantly from George Fox," especially 69.

20. Anstey, *The Atlantic Slave Trade*, 164.

21. Sharp, *Law of Liberty*, 20–21.

22. Davis, *Slavery and Human Progress*, xviii.

biblical arguments could only go so far.[23] Thus Ramsay's 1784 *Essay* aimed to "Prove how much this inconsiderable robbery hurts the master's own interest." Four years later, John Newton's *Journal* drew attention to the moral effect of the slave trade on sailors and traders, as well as the considerable loss of seamen as a result of harsh conditions and violent insurrection. In fact, one of the most effective publications contained no biblical references at all. *An Abstract of the Evidence*, which consisted of data collated by Clarkson and others of the ill treatment of slaves by military officers, sea captains, and doctors, was presented to a Commons select committee in 1791.[24] The evidence spoke for itself.[25]

In the United States, despite the approved disconnection between church and state at Federal level, separation of the biblical and political arguments proved well-nigh impossible.[26] Indeed, the centrality of the Bible in the debate was to be a primary difficulty for the advancement of the abolitionist movement. As Quaker ideas took hold in the North, pro-slavers had to defend their position, and they did so on the basis of Scripture. At first, two themes dominated the argument—race and social order. Quakers insisted on equality—all were children of Adam and Eve (Gen 3:20). Thus, John Woolman warned against treating black people as inferiors.[27] Others, however, argued for "polygenesis"—the idea that blacks were created separately from whites.[28] However, as early as 1700, the puritan Judge Samuel Sewall, citing Psalm 115:16 and Acts 17:26–29, insisted God had made "of one blood all nations." Ultimately, redemption was available to all—black and white alike.[29]

If it had to be conceded that all men were equal, then it could be argued that they were equal but different. The basis for this was the "curse of Ham" in Genesis 9 and 10, which was seen as a prophecy fulfilled in the Negro race. Having seen his father's nakedness, Ham's son Canaan was

23. See Drescher, *Econocide*; Swaminathan, *Debating the Slave Trade*.

24. *An Abstract of the Evidence delivered before a select Committee of the House of Commons in the Years 1790 and 1791 on the Part of the Petitioners for the Abolition of the Slave-Trade*, London, 1791.

25. Hochschild, *Bury the Chains*, 366.

26. Noll, *America's God*, 371.

27. Woolman, *Some Considerations on the Keeping of Negroes*. Despite this, however, it took some time before blacks were accepted as part of the Quaker movement. See Smith, *In His Image*, 35–36.

28. See Kidd, *The Forging of Races*, 149.

29. Sewall, *The Selling of Joseph*.

cursed to be a slave to other nations. The fact that skin color was not mentioned in the text was of course a problem, and various ideas were proposed for its solution. Josiah Priest argued that Ham had been born black—thus the curse of slavery was on those with black skin.[30] John Henry Hopkins, Bishop of Vermont, while declaring himself no lover of slavery, argued that the curse on Ham's progeny was vindicated by the evidence he had found of the degraded way of life in the slave coast of Africa. "In the Providence of God," he wrote, "the negro slavery of the South has been the means of saving millions of those poor creatures from the horrible state in which they must otherwise have lived and died."[31]

Pro-slavers also argued that the South's prosperity was due to its obedience to Scripture. The idea of the conversion and "civilizing" of slaves was seen by many in the South to be part of a healthy, ordered society. Abraham's rule over a household of slaves (e.g., Gen 20:14) was taken as a "model for church and state."[32] If anyone complained that slavery was undemocratic, Southerners like George Fitzhugh responded that "the personal bond between master and slave elevates southern society above northern society," the latter being driven by market forces.[33]

For Thornton Stringfellow, ending slavery would be against the constitution (the "only National constitution which ever emanated directly from God") and amount to "moral hatred" of the laws of God.[34] Slaves were gifts from God; they should be introduced to right religion, just as Israel's slaves were when they were circumcised. In fact, Rev. Fred Ross argued that Scripture actually *commanded* enslavement of others: Leviticus 25:44–46 gave divine sanction to buying slaves from neighboring countries.[35] In the eyes of Southern slave-holders, Scripture was clear: there being no prohibition against slavery, Christians should not presume to invent one. For their part, slaves should accept their station in life and obey God and their masters (Eph 6:5–9; Col 3:22—4:1).

30. Priest, *Slavery, as It Relates to the Negro or African Race*.

31. Hopkins, *A Scriptural, Ecclesiastical, and Historical View of Slavery*, 69.

32. Fox-Genovese and Genovese, *The Mind of the Master Class*, 507.

33. See Morgan, *Slavery in America*, 16. Also Tise, *Proslavery*. On the Southern economy, see Smith, *Debating Slavery*.

34. Thornton Stringfellow in Elliott (ed.), *Cotton is King*, 459–91. On Stringfellow, see Noll *America's God*, 308–9.

35. Ross, *Slavery Ordained of God*, 147.

The argument from social order was not confined to the South. In 1851 the Roman Catholic Bishop Kenrick of Philadelphia published a translation of Paul's letter to Philemon for which he wrote a preface warning that "the Gospel is not directed to disturb the actual order of society by teaching men to disregard their obligations, however severe their enforcement may appear."[36]

Some theologians did attempt to argue against such ideas on the basis of Scripture. Edwardsean "New Divinity" preachers objected to the notion that America had a God-given, biblically sanctioned right to be a slave-holding nation. Samuel Hopkins, for example, tried to tackle the idea that the Bible could be used to support patriotism of this sort, and to show that it was inconsistent to enslave Africans while at the same time asserting their own "civil liberty." He also suggested that the owners' treatment of their slaves was at odds with the biblical teaching to love one's neighbors and care for the strangers and fatherless.[37] Northern voices such as these, however, had little impact on Southern slave-holders, and as the debate gained momentum, it was the argument on the basis of the Golden Rule that stimulated most discussion.[38] Pro-slavers began to argue about its proper interpretation. In a public letter to Rev. Albert Barnes, Ross admitted that the Golden Rule was the strongest argument against slavery. However, "Christ, in his rule,"

> *presupposes* that the man to whom he gives it *knows*, and from the
> Bible, (or providence, or natural conscience, *so far as in harmony*
> with the Bible,) the *various relations* in which God has placed him;

36. Kenrick, *The Acts of the Apostles,* 32. Kenrick's argument from Scripture was consistent with the Roman Catholic position of maintaining the status quo, but unusual in being based on the Bible rather than referring to tradition and papal authority. Prior to the rise of abolitionism the Roman Catholic church had given mixed messages regarding slavery, largely in reaction to situations arising in the mission field. While some individuals and religious orders spoke against it as contrary to the Christian ethic, in general the church's stance was that slavery was the result of the fall, and its continuation in accordance with natural law. Priority was given to the religious instruction of slaves. See Rice, *American Catholic Opinion in the Slavery Controversy,* 11–24; Boxer, *The Church Militant,* 30–38. The place of Catholicism in the history of the American debate is complicated by anti-Catholic prejudice amongst some Protestant abolitionists. See McGreevy, *Catholicism and American Freedom,* 43–47; Maxwell, *Slavery and the Catholic Church*; Hayes, "Reflections on Slavery."

37. Hopkins, *A Dialogue, concerning the slavery of the Africans.* See Noll, "The Image of the United States."

38. For an excellent recent account of the development of the debate see Oshatz, *Slavery and Sin.*

and the *respective duties* in those relations; i.e. The rule *assumes* that he KNOWS what he OUGHT to *expect* or *desire* in similar circumstances.[39]

In other words, the Golden Rule itself is subject to other rules, and only to be called upon when the others had already been applied. With regard to human relations, it may only be referred to when it is recalled that God has ordained them to be conducted within the social confines of marriage, family life, and slave-owning. The Golden Rule should be applied in the light of the law, rather than the other way around. Similarly, Richard Furman, writing for the South Carolina Baptist State Convention in 1822, argued, "Surely this rule is never to be urged against that order of things, which the divine government has established, nor do our desires become a standard to us, under this rule, unless they have due regard to justice, propriety, and the general good."[40] Clearly for Furman, justice, propriety, and the general good meant the continuation of slavery.

At the same time however, there were some who, while holding to the inerrancy of Scripture, did feel uneasy about slaveholding. While the Bible did not allow for abolitionism, it did say that slavery would one day be ended. Rev. Fred Ross was convinced: "God never intended the relation of master and slave to be perpetual."[41] So too, Charles Hodge, professor and later principal of Presbyterian Princeton Theological Seminary, suggested that improving the education and family lives of slaves would lead eventually to emancipation. But Hodge's view, which was widely disseminated through the influential journal *The Biblical Repertory and Princeton Review*, did not allow for change in the current situation. Slavery may not be part of the divine plan, but the fact that neither Jesus nor Paul demanded freedom for slaves meant that involvement in the abolition campaign was a sin against God.[42] One day all slaves would be set free, but the time was not yet. It is more accurate to describe him as anti-abolitionist than anti-slavery, though in practice, Hodge's view probably contributed to the continuation of pro-slavery thinking amongst American Protestants.[43]

---

39. Ross, *Slavery Ordained of God*, 162.

40. Quoted in Callahan, *The Talking Book*, 36.

41. Ross, *Slavery Ordained of God*, 6.

42. Hodge, *View of the Subject of Slavery*. For the idea of progressive revelation in Hodge see his *Systematic Theology* Vol 1, 446. See Torbett *Theology and Slavery*, 6.

43. Contra Tise, *Proslavery*, 278 who sees Hodge as pro-slavery.

Hodge freely admitted that he was primarily concerned to conserve Calvinist theology rather than create new ideas. Following the Scottish "common sense" philosopher Thomas Reid, the Princetonians emphasized the importance of sense experience, while allowing for some innate or intuitive knowledge.[44] Thus the Bible could be seen both as the mysterious "word of God" and as a textbook that gave the kind of data that science could provide. Newtonian law described the world, the Bible contained truth.[45] And as true Enlightenment scholars, they considered it their task to determine what that data was.

Many abolitionists, however, were disturbed by this approach, which played into the pro-slavers' hands.[46] For the Philadelphian Presbyterian minister Albert Barnes, ethos trumped law. Although Jesus did not actually demand the abolition of slavery, the principles of his teaching, and that of the apostles "if carried out, would secure its universal abolition."[47] Horace Bushnell, a Congregationalist minister in Connecticut, believed in a "principle of virtue," and that God could speak to human emotions through poetry and metaphor as well as the intellect.[48] Thus, for academics and many clergy, the issue came to be not so much one's opinion on the matter of slavery, but how one viewed the Bible. The question was whether one should follow the didactic inerrantism characteristic of the Princetonians or a hermeneutic that looked for principles conveyed through narrative and symbol.[49]

But the hermeneutical battle detracted attention from the matter in hand, and it failed to move the abolitionist campaign forward. A major catalyst for change in the North came in 1839 when Theodore D. Weld's *Slavery as It Is: Testimony of a Thousand Witnesses* sold 22,000 copies within four months of publication. Its evidence of the torture and harsh punishments meted out to slaves, taken from reports by slaveholders to Southern newspapers, would, he believed, bring about the judgment of God, the slaveholders being condemned out of their own mouths.[50] The document

44. See Noll, *The Princeton Theology*, 13.

45. Ibid., 39; Kidd, *The Forging of Races*, 83.

46. An edited version of Hodge's essay was included in Elliott's *Cotton is King*; see Torbett, *Theology and Slavery*, 7.

47. Barnes, *An Inquiry*, 340.

48. Torbett, *Theology and Slavery*, 121, 130.

49. Ibid., 15.

50. Weld, *Slavery as It Is*. See Thomas, *Slavery Attacked*, 57–62.

inspired others to join the campaign, the most influential of all being Harriet Beecher Stowe, whose novel *Uncle Tom's Cabin* played a major role in the success of abolitionism. Written in response to the Fugitive Slave Act of 1850, the book appealed to the "genuine universality of feeling, a sense of common humanity."[51] Exploiting the power of sympathy for social change, Stowe dwelt on the sufferings of slaves, in particular, the heartbreak caused by the separation of families. Married to a clergyman and theologically literate herself, she knew the importance of the Bible in the debate, and used sentimentalism not only to spur people into action against slavery, but to promote the principles of love and mercy over biblicist interpretations.[52]

Stowe's narrative captured the nub of the hermeneutical problem. In this scene, Uncle Tom, who has been sold by his masters and separated from his family, is on a river boat heading south to his new owners. Two passengers are overheard talking about what the Bible has to say on the question of slavery. One, a clergyman, declares "It's undoubtedly the intention of Providence that the African race should be servants—kept in a low condition. 'Cursed be Canaan; a servant of servants shall he be,' the Scripture says." The clergyman's confident quotation implies that any disagreement constitutes disobedience to the Bible and therefore God Himself. On the other hand, it is self-evident to his conversation partner ("a tall slender young man, with a face expressive of great feeling and intelligence") that the principle of the Golden Rule trumps this argument: "'All things whatsoever ye would that men should do unto you, do you even so unto them.' I suppose, he added, that is Scripture, as much as 'Cursed be Canaan.'"[53]

Stowe leaves the reader in no doubt—the "grave looking" clergyman is so taken up with proving his point on the basis of biblical "data" that he has lost all compassion. While the virtuous characters proclaim their dependence on God's mercy and grace, the pro-slavers' references to Scripture reveal their ignorance of the true meaning of the gospel. Moreover, throughout the novel, the godly living of Quakers, who care for runaway slaves, and of Uncle Tom himself, who maintains moral integrity and faith

---

51. On the place of literature in the abolitionist campaign, see Lee, *Slavery, Philosophy, and American Literature*; Bell, *Sentimentalism, Ethics and the Culture of Feeling*, 122. On the nature and influence of sentimental literature, see Carey, *British Abolitionism and the Rhetoric of Sensibility*; Fisher, *Hard Facts*, 87–127; Sabiston, "Anglo-American Connections."

52. See Camfield, "The Moral Aesthetics of Sentimentality."

53. Stowe, *Uncle Tom's Cabin*, 115–16.

in the midst of dreadful suffering, indicts those who think that in treating others as property they are acting in obedience to the Scriptures.

The book was hugely successful and influential in the antislavery campaign. Its harrowing tale of slaves' sufferings spoke to people in a way that academics and clerics could not. Stowe not only brought home the message of the cruelty of slavery, she also pointed up the folly of those who defended it on the grounds of obedience to God. By the time the civil war started, the issue with regard to the Bible was not how to uphold its view of slavery, but how to ensure that its message of freedom and equality, which had been so important since the beginning of the nation, might be extended to *all* its citizens.

4. AMERICAN SLAVES AND THE BIBLE

If it took the American public a while to move away from law to a more intuitive approach to interpretation however, the slaves themselves had been adopting this hermeneutic ever since they had been introduced to the Christian Scriptures by their masters.[54] While most were illiterate, they learned Scripture in oral tradition style, drawing strength from its narratives and metaphors. They discovered that all humanity was created free, that the God who required justice would release the oppressed slaves. The parallels between its narratives and their own situation gave them hope. The Joseph narrative provided a rich source of encouragement, as did the gospel's message of redemption. In particular, the exodus narrative told them that their masters, like the Pharaohs, were working against the will of God.[55] In a letter to Rev. Samson Occom in 1774, Phillis Wheatley wrote that she thought the "Love of Freedom" a universal human trait, for "otherwise, perhaps, the Israelites had been less solicitous for their Freedom from Egyptian slavery."[56] The Negroes' oppressors were "our modern Egyptians," and they drew comfort from the gospel. As Julius Lester notes, the slaves

---

54. In 1706 the Puritan Minister Cotton Mather advocated that slaves be taught the Scriptures in preparation for the life to come—little could be done for them in their present state (Mather, *The Negro Christianized*). The evangelical religious revivals of the 1740s to 1780s (the Great Awakening) resulted in the conversion of many slaves to Christianity.

55. Shannon, "An Anti-bellum Sermon," 105–11; Kling, *The Bible in History*, 195–98. See also Thomas, *Romanticism and Slave Narratives*. See also Kidd, *The Great Awakening*.

56. The letter is reproduced in Carretta, *Unchained Voices*, 69.

fashioned their own kind of Christianity, which they turned to for strength in the constant times of need. In the Old Testament story of the enslavement of the Hebrews by the Egyptians, they found their own story. In the figure of Jesus Christ, they found someone who had suffered as they suffered, someone who understood, someone who offered them rest from their suffering.[57]

Not surprisingly, the exodus theme was important for those who tried to rebel. In 1800, in Henrico county in Virginia, two enslaved brothers, Gabriel and Martin, preached that the Israelites were "a type of successful resistance to tyranny; and it was argued, that now, as then, God would stretch forth his arm to save, and would strengthen a hundred to overthrow a thousand."[58]

Denmark Vesey, who led a planned revolt in 1818 in Charleston, South Carolina, also preached this typology. He and his co-conspirators were executed and the education of slaves thereafter prohibited. But African oral tradition, and the expression of religious thought in poetry, sermons, and spiritual songs such as "Let my People go" and "Go Down Moses" were powerful forces. In reaction to the "Bible Christianity" of their masters, the slaves developed a more experiential type of religion centered around biblical stories and gospel themes of love and redemption.[59] The development of this distinctive, intuitive hermeneutic could not be halted.

Meanwhile, slave owners promoted religion to ensure good behavior from their slaves. Besides the kudos of conversions, religious instruction would mean better servants, and ultimately, better business.[60] Slave revolts merely reinforced the belief that obedience to the Bible produced well organized society—Romans 13 taught that legislative authority should be obeyed, and 1 Timothy 6:2–5 warned against sedition. The slaves themselves, however, drew from the same source to "project their own rights and values as human beings."[61] In a sense, the Scriptures of their oppressors allowed them to form their own identity, and to become social critics. Using the same sources as their masters, but reading them from an entirely

---

57. Lester, *To Be a Slave*, 61.

58. Cited in Harding, "Religion and Resistance," 112 note 15.

59. Callahan, *The Talking Book*; Raboteau, *Slave Religion*, 239–43; Wimbush, "The Bible and African Americans." On slave resistance see Craton, *Testing the Chains*.

60. See, for example the extract from Affleck, "Duties of Overseers."

61. Genovese, *Roll Jordan Roll*, 7.

different viewpoint, slaves found texts that told them that their situation was against the will of God, and promised their vindication.

Slave Narratives

The education of slaves backfired on slaveholders in another way. The testimonies of those who had personal experience of slavery and were now free were highly influential, and not only in the United States.[62] In Britain, slave narratives sold in huge numbers, and their accounts of abuse shamed readers. Students of Oloudah Equiano's *Interesting Narrative*, for example, were horrified to learn that it was "almost a constant practice with our clerks, and other whites, to commit violent depredations on the chastity of the female slaves," and that sailors gratified their "brutal passion with females not yet ten years old."[63] Ignatius Sancho, an African who was brought to Britain on a slave ship in 1731, deplored the failure of the British to live up to their Christian principles. In a letter in 1778, he wrote, "I must observe that your country's conduct has been uniformly wicked in the east West Indies—and even on the coast of Guinea.—The grand object of English navigators—indeed of all Christian navigators—is money—money —money." Although money in itself was not, he conceded, a bad thing, he deplored "the Christians' abominable Traffic for slaves—and the horrid cruelty and treachery of the petty Kings."[64]

The writers of slave narratives showed the British public that, despite widely held beliefs, Africans could be highly cultured and pious. Not only that, they knew their Scriptures. For example, here Equiano relates a conversation he had with a slave:

> One day he said to me, very movingly, "Sometimes when a white man take away my fish, I go to my master, and he get me my right; and when my master, by strength, take away my fishes, what me must do? I can't go to anybody to be righted"; then, said the poor man, looking up above, "I must look up to God Mighty in the top for right." This artless tale moved me much, and I could not help

62. See Phillips, "Slave Narratives."

63. Equiano, *The Interesting Narrative*, 104, 201. See also Fisch, *American Slaves in Victorian England*.

64. In Carretta, *Unchained Voices*, 86.

feeling the just cause Moses had in redressing his brother against the Egyptian.[65]

This analogical hermeneutic, which also characterized the spirituals and writings of American slaves, fueled the realization that slavery was contrary to Christian principles. Like Joseph, Cuobna Ottobah Cuguano, who had been brought by his owner to England in 1772, could see that something evil had been turned round for good (Gen 50:20), but he was also fully aware of the ability of some to back up their pro-slavery by "inconsistent and diabolical use of the sacred writings."[66]

The Old Testament was not to be taken literally, but symbolically, and in the light of the New, which revealed the spiritual nature of the law. Its ideas pointed readers towards the will of God for his people. Frederick Douglass drew on the concept of the image of God to argue for the equal status of the enslaved.

> The slave is a man, "the image of God," but a "little lower than the angels"; possessing a soul, eternal and indestructible; capable of endless happiness, or immeasurable woe.... The first work of slavery is to mar and deface those characteristics of its victims which distinguish men from things and persons from property.[67]

Slave narratives shamed readers into examining their behavior and attitudes towards the colonies. Drawing on familiar biblical images, metaphors, and narratives, they spoke the language of the ordinary churchgoer, and showed the British public just how incompatible with Christianity the treatment of slaves was. The combination of personal experience and the appeal to biblical narrative and ethos was a powerful weapon in the popular antislavery campaign.

5. THE CONTEXT OF THE SLAVERY DEBATE

The ideas and arguments outlined above developed over some 200 years, and while it is true to say that abolitionism was mainly a religious movement, anti-slavery thinking was not confined to the church, nor did the

---

65. Equiano, *The Interesting Narrative*, 110.

66. Cuguano, *Thoughts and Sentiments on the Evil and Wicked Traffic*, 150–60 (156). See further Richards, "The Joseph Story as Slave Narrative." Also Saillant, "Origins of African American Hermeneutics."

67. See Ruston, *Human Rights and the Image of God*, 269.

change of thinking emerge in a vacuum. Its growth was concurrent with, and partly a result of, the development of ideas of freedom and individualism that was taking place in the realms of politics and philosophy. These developments had a direct effect, not only on how slavery was viewed, but also on how Scripture was interpreted.

Philosophical Influences

Although political changes did not take place until the nineteenth century, and religiously motivated campaigning only really took off in the eighteenth, philosophers had been questioning the acceptability of slavery for some time. As early as 1576 the French philosopher Jean Bodin had argued against the idea that slavery was natural simply because of its ubiquity: human sacrifice was also ubiquitous, but no one would say that it was natural. Slavery had had catastrophic effects, bringing about insurrection and revolution on the one hand, and cruelty on the other.[68] In the 1700s, Voltaire (1764) saw slavery as a "degradation of the species" while Montesquieu (1748) took it as read that all men were born equal.[69] Slavery, he said,

> is not good by its nature; it is useful neither to the master nor to the slave: not to the slave, because he can do nothing from virtue; not to the master, because he contracts all sorts of bad habits from his slaves, because he imperceptibly grows accustomed to failing in all the moral virtues, because he grows proud, curt, harsh, angry, voluptuous and cruel.[70]

At the same time, Hobbes's concept of social hierarchy was losing ground and John Locke's idea that each individual has inalienable rights over his or her own life was becoming increasingly influential.[71] Scottish Enlightenment thinkers also began to question the notion that some people should be considered beyond the pale.[72] Francis Hutcheson endorsed Lockean libertarianism, and denounced slavery in his *A System of Moral*

---

68. Bodin, *Six Books of the Commonwealth,* 14–18. Reproduced in Engerman et al., *Slavery,* 15–18.

69. Voltaire "A Philosophical Dictionary" (1764), in Engerman et al., *Slavery,* 24–25.

70. De Montesquieu, *The Spirit of the Laws,* 246–52, in Engerman et al., *Slavery,* 20–23.

71. See *Two Treatises of Government* 2T.2.4; 2T.2.6 (1690). For an introduction to Locke's thought see McCann "John Locke."

72. See Broadie, *The Scottish Enlightenment,* 1997.

Philosophy (1755). In *The Wealth of Nations* (1776) Adam Smith argued that free waged labor was superior to slave labor. The ideas became powerful. In 1791 Thomas Paine, a founding member of the American antislavery society, published his *Rights of Man* which argued for the separation of church and state, against hereditary government, for the natural equality of mankind, and free speech.[73]

Hermeneutical Changes

In such an atmosphere the Quaker movement could grow and flourish. Holding freedom and equality as central tenets, they rebelled against formal religion and developed their own view of Scripture. Largely uneducated, and excluded from the British university system, Quakers denied the need for trained clergy, and even permitted women to preach. Each individual could experience God, and anyone with the "light within," which was available to all, could interpret the Bible. The emphasis on the Spirit accorded the Scriptures a much lower status than in the rest of the Protestant world, and they were suspected of denying the authority of the word of God.[74] While their values could be shown to have biblical basis, however, this did not render its members immune to censure and even persecution. As the clergyman John Stalham wrote, the Quakers had "a zeal for God but not according to knowledge."[75]

In contrast, evangelicals on both sides of the Atlantic considered theological education to be very important indeed. British clergy were taught in universities, and in America, Protestant denominations vied with each other in setting up seminaries for the training of their ministers. At the same time, the universities were embracing rationalist ideas which directly affected the way the Bible was interpreted. The idea that reason, rather than superstition and speculation, could bring an understanding of the world was appealing to those of Puritan heritage and was rapidly taking hold.[76] German universities in particular began to eschew the notion of the supernatural in the study of the Bible, and historical-critical methods became

---

73. On eighteenth-century thought on slavery see Anstey, *The Atlantic Slave Trade*, 91–125.

74. See Hill, *The World Turned Upside Down*, 261–68.

75. In his *The Contradictions of the Quakers to the Scriptures of God* (1655) quoted in Moore, *The Light in their Consciences*, 103.

76. On the Puritan mindset see Reventlow, *The Authority of the Bible*, 93–184.

increasingly influential. However, evangelicals remained suspicious of the hyper-rationality of the German approach which seemed to rule out the view that the Scriptures were the very word of God himself. Intellectual developments on the Continent were to be welcomed, but with caution.

Cultural Influences

Biblical interpretation was also affected by changes that were taking place in the literary world. The writers and artists known to us now as the Romantics, while steeped in biblical language, looked to the Christian Scriptures not for information, but for their ideas and spirituality. Reacting against rationalist and reductionist tendencies, they looked for "the similar ordering or structure" between their world and that of the Bible from which inferences might be drawn.[77] Biblical typology, analogy, and symbolism could help them understand human experience. Poetry and the relatively new genre of the novel allowed interpreters to retain some of the spiritual mystery of scriptural teaching without relapsing into medieval Catholic allegorical interpretation, or the mechanistic thinking that was characteristic of continental scholarship.[78] According to Coleridge, for example, the Bible was designed for the "moral and spiritual Education of the Human Race."[79] *Wissenschaft* was stifling; it led readers away from human relationships and the deeper reality which sense experience alone could not disclose.

However, while values of freedom and equality could be seen as congruent with Scripture, good biblical interpreters also wanted to show that their interpretation was rational, based on evidence. This approach was important to the academics and clerics of the Princeton school, who were strongly influenced by Scottish common sense philosophy. Unfortunately, as we have seen, this emphasis played into the hands of pro-slavers who wanted to preserve the status quo. What could be more rational than upholding the law? But while academics and clerics argued over the niceties of biblical interpretation, and clung to the literal meaning of certain areas of the text, slaves and the general public took a more intuitive, experiential

77. Harris, "Allegory to Analogy in the Interpretation of Scriptures"; see also Deconinck-Brossard, "England and France in the Eighteenth Century," 136–81; Wedd "Literature and Religion."

78. Deconinck-Brossard, "England and France," 201.

79. CL V 372 quoted in Davidson, "S. T. Coleridge," 416. See Jasper, *The Sacred and Secular Canon* on the role of the canon in Romanticism in general.

view, on which Romanticism and sentimentalism could build. These two hermeneutical approaches were at odds and became increasingly so as the campaign developed. As the general public listened to the tales, poetry, and songs that drew on the metaphors, narratives, and principles of Scripture, the interpretative approach that came so naturally to the slaves themselves spoke much more powerfully than any appeal to law.

6. DIFFERENCES ACROSS THE ATLANTIC

These developments and influences were at work on both sides of the Atlantic, but why did the course of the debate take such different forms in Britain and America? There are some obvious differences: the issue of slavery was much more personal to most Americans, while it was far removed from most Britons.[80] Given the importance of slavery for their way of life and livelihood, particularly in the South, it is unsurprising that slaveowners should battle for its continuation. Furthermore, as we have seen, many American slaveholders sincerely believed that slaveholding was biblically sanctioned—God had given them land and slaves, just as he had given them to Abraham and the patriarchs. Naturally, such views brought about powerful reactions. The Puritans had themselves been trying to escape the tyranny of the church, and they thought of the biblical exodus as a type of their own journey into a promised land.[81] With such ideas rooted deep in white American psyche, when crisis came and questions were raised about the nature of that freedom, the Bible played a central role, in a way that was quite different from Britain.

The fact that slaves found in the Bible reason to defy their masters increased the hermeneutical divide. And while liberal clergy built up their intellectual attack on the pro-slavery stance, some, such as the radical abolitionist Lloyd Garrison, were so horrified by it that they jettisoned the Bible altogether. In the end, however, Garrison's approach played into the hands of the slaveholders; Scripture was too important in American thinking to be disregarded.[82] The hermeneutical debate was polarized in a way that it never was in Britain.

---

80. Anstey, *The Atlantic Slave Trade*, 192; Noll, *The Civil War as a Theological Crisis*, 122–23.

81. Reventlow, *The Authority of the Bible*, 141.

82. Noll, *The Civil War as Theological Crisis*, 32.

Secondly, the question of race was not as critical in Britain as it was in America. The campaigners in Britain did not have to contend with arguments regarding the biblical status of the black slave. Hannah More's *Slavery: A Poem* argued that Africans were made in the image of God and had the same feelings as Europeans, intentionally refuting the arguments of Hume and others that Africans were inferior to whites.[83] Cowper's poem *Charity* asked directly:

> Canst thou, and honoured with a Christian name,
> Buy what is woman-born, and feel no shame?

This points to another major difference. Much of the American debate was carried out by clerics and academics. In Britain, however, the main protagonists were politicians and writers. Powerful literary voices like those of Newton, More, and Cowper contributed to the campaign by writing poems and hymns. All of these writers were influenced by Romanticism, whose values of individualism, democracy, and human sympathy were highly compatible with the anti-slavery cause.[84]

American academics, on the other hand, were fighting over biblical interpretation. Indeed, the Princetonians and others were battling on several fronts at once—abolitionism being secondary to defending their inerrantism against domestic liberalism and European hyper-rationalism. Moreover, after the 1820s, when Coleridge's *Aids to Reflection* arrived in America, Romantic ideas became suspect too. The American abolitionist Lydia Maria Child published some of Blake's *Songs* for a wide readership in 1842. And as these ideas spread, they challenged the prevailing evangelical biblical hermeneutic.[85] For readers such as Horace Bushnell, Romanticism offered a different way of looking at the Bible from the dominant Edwardsean thinking, which for some had become sterile and legalistic. But the Princetonians held on to the idea of a literal view of Scripture and attacked

---

83. Stott, *Hannah More*, 92–94. On evangelicalism in the abolitionist cause in the UK and America see Wolffe, *The Expansion of Evangelicalism*, chapter 7. For a selection of poetry from the period see Wood, *The Poetry of Slavery*.

84. The high ideals of abolitionism, combined with an interest in exoticism and what Alan Richardson calls the "overvaluation of racial and cultural differences," made antislavery attractive to Romantic writers (Richardson, "Slavery and Romantic Writers"). See also Cranston, *The Romantic Movement*; Lee, *Slavery and the Romantic Imagination*.

85. On the influence of Coleridge's *Aids to Reflection* see Ledbetter, "Changing Sensibilities." On Coleridge and the Bible see Reardon, *Religious Thought in the Victorian Age*, 43–61.

thinkers like Bushnell for undermining the authority of Scripture and prizing emotion over reason.[86]

Such battles had not concerned Wilberforce and his colleagues. While Presbyterians, Unitarians, and others supported the cause, the Clapham group was mainly Anglican. For them, the Bible was an *external* authority—the "blessed repository of heavenly truth and consolation."[87] In Lockean manner, they held that religion was a matter of reason, and that Scripture provided rational guidance for living.[88] But central to their faith was the need for a practical response to the gift of salvation, which was available to all. Thus, "whatever hindered salvation, whether ignorance, penal laws, factory conditions, or slavery, had to be remedied or removed."[89] And they were well aware of the irony of believing that they had experienced freedom through the atoning death of Christ while supporting the enslavement of others.[90] As Anstey writes,

> For the Evangelical, slavery stood particularly condemned. This was because he apprehended salvation not least through the concept of redemption, and when he related the role of redemption, in its existential, individual application, to God's great redemptive purpose as made known in the Old Testament, he saw that, historically, redemption was release from physical bondage as well as from sin.[91]

This of course could also be said of many American evangelicals, but the difference is that the British Anglicans were not heirs of the strict biblicist view that grew up in certain parts of American Protestantism and that drove a wedge between most evangelicals and the Quakers. Amongst the Clapham Sect a Latitudinarian concern for the practical outcome of faith meant that collaboration with the Quakers, whose works so influenced

---

86. Minkema and Stout, "The Edwardsean Tradition and the Antislavery Debate"; Torbett, *Theology and Slavery*, 137.

87. Sheehan, *The Enlightenment Bible*, 246. Quote from Wilberforce's *A Practical View of the Prevailing Religious System*, 13.

88. Bebbington, *Evangelicalism in Modern Britain*, 48–56.

89. Cowherd, *The Politics of English Dissent*, 47.

90. On the history and nature of evangelicalism see Bebbington, *Evangelicalism in Modern Britain*. For discussion of Bebbington see Haykin and Stewart *The Emergence of Evangelicalism*. On the idea of abolitionism as atoning for the nation's sins see Hilton, *The Age of Atonement*, 209. See also Barclay "Am I Not a Man and a Brother?"

91. Anstey, "Religion and British Slave Emancipation," 40.

Clarkson and Sharp, was much less of a problem.[92] Whether the hermeneutical starting point was spiritual redemption or religious freedom, each could see that all men and women were born equal under God, and that this rendered slavery incompatible with Christianity. Once convinced of the sufferings involved in slavery, they had to admit that the behavior of British slaveholders was irreconcilable with their idea of what Christianity (and being British) was about.

7. CONCLUSION

The Bible played a pivotal role in the development of abolitionist thinking. From the beginning, the Quakers looked to the Golden Rule as fundamental in the argument against slavery. Eventually, this way of thinking became the hermeneutical key for the antislavery campaign as a whole. Despite the fact that Levitical law permitted slavery, despite the fact that neither Jesus nor Paul had repealed that law, the view that slavery was incompatible with divine love prevailed. However, the change that took place did not come easily, and there was a marked difference in its course between America and the United Kingdom. In Britain, any biblicist voice was quickly undermined, as the Quakers and evangelicals were able to work together for a common cause. But if the Bible was a motivational and reliable guide for the campaigners, it remained at that level, and did not, in the end, play a major role in the political debates that culminated in changing the law.

In the United States, the Bible was central because of the place it held in the collective psyche. Northerners and Southerners alike knew their Bibles inside out. Most Americans held fast to the view that they had been given the land by God himself, and slaveholders believed the same about their slaves. Thus when the Quaker attack came, it was only natural that the debate should feature claims and counter-claims based on Scripture. Ultimately, of course, political and social change came about only after civil war. But in the run up to that war, the biblical arguments became more complex and in the end proved self-defeating. The law of love held sway, over and above the inerrantism of the Princetonians and attempts of Southern slaveholders to preserve their way of life as God-given. And in fact, it took a sentimental novelist to bring the follies of the argument to public

---

92. Drescher, "Public Opinion and the Destruction of British Colonial Slavery." On Latitudinarianism, see Reventlow, *Authority of the Bible*, 223–85.

notice and to convince many that the law of love was a more powerful maxim than any overt scriptural statement about slavery.

What were the hermeneutical approaches? Broadly speaking, there were two. The Quakers' internalized, intuitive hermeneutic was adopted by many for whom the stark evidence of suffering and injustice meant that things had to change. On the other hand, there were those who looked for law, and the biblicists who looked to the Bible for data for living. For those for whom the Bible was "an omnicompetent infallible authority for life now and forever,"[93] the intuitive focus on ideas of love and redemption, rather than quoting chapter and verse, seemed to be disingenuous and subversive. They may have embraced contemporary ideals of freedom and equality but these had to be seen within the constraints of their interpretation of Scripture.

Both sides made use of typology and prophecy; abolitionists and slaveholders alike drew illuminative analogies between biblical narratives and their own situations. Rationalism and "common sense" philosophy informed each side of the debate, but the Romantics, and popular sentimentalists, bolstered the antislavery cause with powerful effect. For the antislavery proponents, and slaves themselves, the ethos embedded in biblical narratives, not least the central story of the gospel itself, inspired courage and the impetus to work for change. And in the end, the legalism and biblicism that seemed so authoritative and foolproof to so many proved impotent in the face of the evidence of the reality of peoples' lives, and the need to change that reality for the better.

93. Noll, *America's God*, 397.

CHAPTER 3

The Bible and Slavery

1. INTRODUCTION

The abolitionist success meant that the Christian view of slavery changed. Slavery, however, did not go away, and of course, the worldview of the Bible remains the same. So the question arises— what, if anything, can it contribute to a Christian response to contemporary human trafficking? To answer this question, we will now turn to the biblical literature itself, and in order to bridge the hermeneutical gap between the biblical era and our own, we will draw on lessons learned from the story of the Bible in the abolitionist campaign. Like the abolitionists, we are confronted with the injustice and cruelty of human trafficking, and like them we know that it is incompatible with what we know of the love of God. So, like them, we come to the Bible with an agenda—a desire for change, a desire to see the ending of injustice and the alleviation of suffering. Moreover, we have seen that the prescriptive, literalist approach relied on by the pro-slavers was ultimately self-serving and counter-productive. Therefore, we will come to the text, consciously adopting the hermeneutic of "moral intuition" which was so effective for social change.[1] In other words, we are setting out to try to discern the "spirit" of the biblical literature regarding

1. Harrill, "The Use of the New Testament in the American Slave Controversy."

slavery, an overall ethos that bears witness to the story of God's dealings with humanity, rather than the "letter of the law."

However, adopting this approach demands that some further questions be addressed. First, considerable advances have been made in biblical studies since the time of the abolitionists—does their approach stand up to scrutiny today—or must it be dismissed as a wishful and idealistic, even a dishonest use of Scripture? Second, what are we to do with the texts that seem to be so at odds with the law of love and with our contemporary view of slavery?

With all this in mind, we will now conduct a survey of those passages that deal with slavery—first in the Old Testament and then in the New. We will rely to a great extent on recent social-scientific criticism, which allows us insights into the social world in which the writers of the texts lived and their reasons for writing as they did.[2] Besides looking at the legal material, which was so central to the debates in the eighteenth century, we will consider other biblical passages that mention slavery, taking into account their literary genres and purpose, before drawing our findings together in an attempt to outline a canonical perspective of slavery that might inform a discussion of human trafficking today.

2. SLAVERY IN THE OLD TESTAMENT

The Legal Collections

The existence of slavery is assumed throughout the Old Testament. Abraham, Isaac, and Jacob were slave-owners (Gen 12:16; 26:19; 30:43). According to Numbers 31, Moses commanded that slaves be taken in the Midianite campaign. It is likely that most slaves in ancient Israel were non-nationals, taken either from neighboring countries or from among foreigners living temporarily in the land (Lev 25:44–46) and that they were used in domestic or agricultural work.[3] Foreigners were used as slave labor

---

2. Pleins, *The Social Visions of the Hebrew Bible*, 20: "In bridging between sociological analysis and ethics, it is the task of the contemporary interpreter to ensure that historical models and sociological theories are employed to clarify the nature and character of biblical social ethics in its social world both as an integrative as well as a generative force."

3. The term *'ebed* (male slave) is fluid, its meaning ranging from chattel slave to a general designation of lower rank, for example in the royal court (e.g., 2 Sam 9:2; 15:14–15). This makes deciding whether chattel or debt slavery is being considered in any given

in national building projects (e.g., 1 Kgs 9:22; 2 Chr 2:17–18; 8:7–9), and as temple servants (Num 31:30, 47). The law collections contain evidence of attempts to legislate against cruelty and abuse. For example, if a slave died as a result of a beating by his master, the master was to be punished (Exod 21:20). Slaves who were injured were to go free (Exod 21:26). In an ordinance unique in the ancient Near East, fugitive slaves were to be given asylum (Deut 23:15–16).[4]

Some destitute Hebrews sold themselves and their families into debt bondage in order to survive, a practice that was discouraged.[5] Deuteronomic law instructs that those in debt-bondage were to be freed in the seventh year (Exod 21:2; Deut 15:12) and given plentiful supplies to begin the new phase in their lives. In Levitical law, those in debt-bondage were to be considered as hired servants rather than slaves (Lev 25:39–40), and to be released in the year of Jubilee (Lev 25:40). It was recognized that some slaves might not wish to leave their masters, and in such instances, a public ceremony was prescribed (Exod 21:5–6; Deut 15:16–18) in which the servant's ear was to be pierced with an awl. Hebrews were not to be sold to foreigners (Lev 25:42), and the families of those who had to sell themselves were expected to redeem their relatives (Lev 25:47–52). According to the Holiness Code, they too were to be released in the year of Jubilee.[6]

The disapproval of debt-bondage was closely related to legislation designed to protect Hebrews from extreme poverty and against corruption or abuse of power (e.g., the statute against usury in Lev 25:35–38).[7] There was a responsibility to care for the poor and needy, at both judicial and individual levels. This included the good treatment of hired servants (Deut 24:14–15), and the prohibition of kidnap and dishonest financial transactions (Deut 24:7; 25:13–16; Lev 19:35–37). Even the king was accountable to Yahweh, and subject to the laws of the land (Deut 17:14–20).

The slave laws are preserved in three major legal collections, which come from different times and schools of thought (Exod 21; Lev 25; and

---

passage problematic. See Botterweck et al., *TDOT* Vol. X, 387–404. For an overview of Old Testament slavery see Haas, "Slave, Slavery"; Matthews and Benjamin, *Social World of Ancient Israel*, 199–210. See also Jackson, *Wisdom Laws*, 79–119.

4. On the laws of surrounding ANE nations see Dandamaev, "Slavery (ANE)"; Jackson, "Biblical Laws of Slavery."

5. On debt bondage in Israel see Chirichigno, *Debt-Slavery in Israel.*

6. On the Jubilee year see Wright, "Jubilee, Year of"; Ringe "Jubilee, Year of." See also Westbrook, *Property and the Family in Biblical Law*, 36–57; Amit, "The Jubilee Law."

7. See Hoppe, *There Shall Be No Poor among You*, 17–42.

Deut 15). This helps account for various differences between them, for example, with regard to the release of slaves. Indeed, we should not see Old Testament law as a "monolithic code," valid at all stages in Israel's history. For the collections reflect layers of development and change over centuries—the preserved accumulation of a process that was trying to find "the best life possible."[8]

Moreover, legal codes can, at best, only give us some idea of the kind of society law-makers would like to see, they do not describe what actually goes on in society.[9] This disparity is illustrated in the Bible itself. For example, despite the injunctions against enslaving one's kinsmen, Hebrews were drafted in for compulsory service (corvée) by their own rulers. Nehemiah may have expressed outrage at the poverty that drove some to sell their children because of famine (Neh 5:1–5) and the usury that contributed to such suffering, but he also enlisted men and their servants to expedite the rebuilding of the Jerusalem wall (Neh 4:16–22). Solomon, who required a work force for his building projects, had large numbers of men working in mines and foundries (1 Kgs 5:13–15). After his death, increased demands placed on these workers by his son led to rebellion (1 Kgs 12).

Nor should we infer that slavery in ancient Israel was essentially benign compared with later slave systems. Slavery may not have been systematized in the manner of antebellum America, but it was still inherently unjust and cruel.[10] As in all slave labor, the wellbeing of the individual slave and his family depended on the disposition of the master. But as Orlando Patterson has shown, slavery involves much more than the risk of severe physical punishment. It means removal from all one knows ("natal alienation") and being robbed of one's identity.[11] The laws concerning debt-bondage may have offered some protection to Hebrews facing destitution, but foreigners captured in war were removed from their homes and families. Forcible

8. Harrill, "Slavery," 302; Fretheim, "Law in the Service of Life." On OT law in general see Selman, "Law"; Matthews, "The Anthropology of Slavery in the Covenant Code"; Marshall, *Israel and the Book of the Covenant*; Fishbane, *Biblical Interpretation in Ancient Israel*, 91–277. For an overview of the discussion regarding dating and sources see Harrelson, *Hebrew Bible*, 17–18, 25–28, 57–61. See also Moshe Weinfeld's *The Place of the Law in the Religion of Ancient Israel*.

9. Harrill, *The Manumission of Slaves*, 14.

10. *Pace* Kaiser, *Toward Old Testament Ethics*, 98, who declares that slavery in OT times was "not the horrible institution known by the same name in modern western countries."

11. Patterson, *Slavery and Social Death*, 13.

acculturation, such as circumcision and participation in the cult, may not have been welcomed by the slaves themselves.[12] Nevertheless, a concern for human dignity and freedom is detectable throughout the law collections.[13] For example, the suffering of those taken in war is acknowledged explicitly in Deuteronomy 21:10–14, in which women in this situation are given time to mourn the loss of their family. They are accorded the status of wives (or concubines) in the household, and protected from being sold as chattel slaves.[14] Similarly, the laws against abuse, and the concept of the Jubilee, bear witness to this ethos.

Certainly, with respect to freeing slaves, Israel may have been no different from her near neighbors. For example, legislation for the release of debt-slaves was also found in the cuneiform laws.[15] However, what made Hebrew law distinctive was its theological basis, which is reiterated throughout the collections.[16] The slave laws were underpinned by the belief that all human beings are made in the image of God. While chattel slaves were considered to be of less (monetary) value than free Hebrews (see, e.g., Exod 21:28–32), the belief in the inherent dignity of human beings is reflected in statutes requiring that masters should not maim or mutilate their servants (Exod 21:26–27).[17]

Most important, however, was the collective memory of Israel's own deliverance from oppression, encapsulated in the exodus story. In Egypt, the Israelites had been subjected to forced labor (corvée) rather than chattel slavery, but their humiliation and oppression was slavery as far as they were concerned, and the exodus became pivotal for their self-understanding and sense of identity (Exod 1:11).[18] They must never forget that Yahweh had delivered them, and made a covenant of love with them (e.g., Exod 20:2; Deut 7:6–11; 8:11–20).[19] The exodus underpinned the disapproval of debt-bondage (Lev 25:39; Deut 15:12): the Israelite did not, could not, belong to

12. Cf. Bennett, *Injustice Made Legal.*

13. Weinfeld, *Deuteronomy and the Deuteronomic School*, 282ff.

14. The laws concerning female slaves will be considered further in chapter 5.

15. See Westbrook, "Slave and Master in Ancient Near Eastern Law."

16. Weinfeld, *Social Justice in Ancient Israel*, 11.

17. Baker, *Tight Fists or Open Hands?* 128; Wright, *Old Testament Ethics for the People of God*, 337.

18. On the relationship between law and exodus see Daube, *The Exodus Pattern in the Bible*; Urbach, *The Laws Regarding Slavery*; Callender, "Servants of God(s) and Servants of Kings," 78.

19. Wright, *Old Testament Ethics*, 27, 38.

anyone other than Yahweh (Lev 25:55). It informed the instructions that resident aliens be treated humanely (Deut 24:17–18). Yahweh had responded to the suffering of his people (Exod 3:7–8a), and Hebrews must imitate Him.[20] Thus, Sabbath and festival observance applied to one's servants too (Exod 20:10; Deut 5:14; 12:12; 16:11), and freed slaves should be given provisions, just as the Hebrews had been given silver when they left Egypt (Deut 15:13–15).[21]

The freedom afforded by the exodus, therefore, was not unlimited (Exod 20:3–5). When God liberated them it was the victory of one king over another, one master over another (Lev 25:55).[22] Their freedom carried with it the responsibility to look out for the wellbeing of the neighbor and the prevention of corruption and oppression of the weak and the poor.

Slavery in the Prophets and Writings

The values with regard to slavery expressed in the legal collections are found throughout the Old Testament literature. In the Pentateuch, besides the exodus narrative, the Joseph story gives a message that to be a slave does not rob the individual of dignity or break the relationship between oneself and God. Later narratives, such as that of the slave girl who enables Naaman to be healed (2 Kgs 5), similarly highlight slaves' inherent humanity. As in the story of Abraham's servant in Genesis 24, whose faithfulness to Yahweh ensures that Rebekah becomes his master's wife, they tell of slaves who are used by God, and given divine guidance.[23]

Wisdom literature speaks of slaves in a common-sense manner. It is acknowledged that slaves can be wise and shrewd (Prov 17:2), but at the same time there is a need to understand one's place in society (e.g., Eccl 10:5–7; Prov 19:10; 30:22) and to deal with servants sensibly (Prov 30:10). According to Job 31:13–15, the just treatment of slaves is a natural part of an ethical life under Yahweh.[24]

---

20. Nasuti, "Identity, Identification and Imitation"; Birch, *Let Justice Roll Down*, 119, 125.

21. See Carmichael, *Law and Narrative in the Bible*, 82.

22. Callender, "Servants of God(s)," 78; Levenson, *The Hebrew Bible*, 140; Radner, *Leviticus*, 272; Eslinger, "Freedom or Knowledge?"

23. See Teugels, "The Anonymous Matchmaker."

24. See Neville, "A Reassessment of the Radical Nature of Job's Ethic."

In the prophets, as in the legal collections, ideas of freedom and dignity are closely related to concern for the poor and curtailing corruption and oppression (e.g., Jer 22:13–19; Mal 3:5). Moral decline could be traced to forgetting that Yahweh had brought them out of Egypt (Amos 2:10; 3:1; 9:7; Hos 13:4–6; Mic 6:2–8).[25] The fact that there was debt-slavery at all was an outrage to the eighth-century prophets—Amos and Micah were opposed to it.[26] When the principle of a seven-year release was ignored, Jeremiah had to intervene—there was to be no exploitation of fellow Hebrews (Jer 34:12–16).[27] Joel denounced those nations that had reduced the people of Jerusalem and Judah to items of trade (Joel 3:1–6). Boys and girls have been traded for prostitutes and wine, and sent far away from home. Such shameful violation of Yahweh's people deserves to be punished, and Yahweh threatens to do the same to them.[28]

Isaiah envisaged a new peaceful exodus (e.g., 43:16–21; 51:9–11) brought about by the suffering slave (*'ebed*) who would bring not only Israel, but all the nations, back to God (42:1–4; 49:1–6; 50:4–9; 52:13—53:12).[29] Israel must treat others in the way that she had been treated by God, thus becoming an example to the nations (Isa 40–66). They must take "God's character as the pattern of their character and God's deeds as the model for theirs."[30] In practice, there might be social divisions, but before God, all human distinctions ultimately break down (Isa 24:2).

Conclusion on the Old Testament and Slavery

Implicit in the law collections are underlying values of freedom (for Hebrews in the first instance) and human dignity.[31] The laws themselves

25. Wright, *Old Testament Ethics*, 44. Collins, "The Exodus and Biblical Theology." On the relationship between prophecy and Law see Tucker, "The Law in the Eighth Century Prophets."

26. Dearman, *Property Rights in the Eighth Century Prophets*, 54.

27. On the relationship between Jeremiah and Leviticus see Leuchter, "The Manumission Laws in Leviticus and Deuteronomy."

28. Crenshaw, *Joel*, 182–83; Wolff, *Joel and Amos*, 77.

29. Zenger, "The God of Exodus in the Message of the Prophets"; Anderson "Exodus and Covenant in Second Isaiah and Prophetic Tradition"; Hugenberger, "The Servant of the Lord in the 'Servant Songs' of Isaiah."

30. Barton, "The Basis of Ethics in the Hebrew Bible," 17; Birch, "Divine Character and the Formation of Moral Community"; Hubbard, "The Divine Redeemer."

31. Snell, *Flight and Freedom in the Ancient Near East*, 117–36.

belong to particular times and places, and were never intended to provide blanket rules for undifferentiated application. As Richard Bauckham says, their purpose was not so much to legislate as "to educate the people in the will of God for the whole of their life as his people, to create and develop the conscience of the community."[32] So too, the laws must be seen against the backdrop of the story of God's dealings with his people.[33] The most powerful expression of God's concern for liberation of the oppressed is, of course, the exodus narrative, but this message is found throughout the Prophets and the Writings too. God's demand that others be treated justly is a consistent motif throughout the whole of the Old Testament canon.

3. SLAVERY IN THE NEW TESTAMENT

As in the Hebrew Bible, so in the New—the existence of slavery is assumed to be the norm. The Greco-Roman world, in which the New Testament writers lived and worked, was a rigidly stratified society in which the difference between masters and slaves was stark. Slaves were, quite simply, the lowest of the low. Some became slaves as a result of being captured in war, but many others were born into captivity. The practice of exposing unwanted children provided many slaves.

Although most slaves lived and worked in intolerable conditions, some could become influential, developing skills and knowledge indispensable to their masters and even sometimes able to earn money and keep slaves of their own. Nevertheless, even they were considered to be non-persons, inferior beings, with no civic rights. Their families and their bodies were considered the sole property of their masters, who had absolute rights over them. In a society in which all free men were driven to seek and maintain honor, the status of the slave could only be one of shame. Manumission was regularly practised—but this was double-edged, for as well as holding out the hope of freedom, it encouraged slaves to work well for their masters, thus perpetuating the system.[34]

32. Bauckham, *The Bible in Politics*, 26; also Nicholson, "Deuteronomy's Vision of Israel"; Phillips, *The Laws of Slavery*; Goldingay, *Old Testament Theology*, 39.

33. On the crucial link between law and narrative see Janzen, *Exodus*; Watts, *Reading Law*.

34. On the nature of Greco-Roman slavery see Finley, *Classical Slavery*; Westermann, *The Slave Systems of Greek and Roman Antiquity*; Wiedemann, *Slavery*; Jeremias, *Jerusalem in the Time of Jesus*, 110–11, 312–16.

As the earliest Christian communities developed in this environment, it was natural that the language of slavery would feature strongly in their attempts at understanding themselves, their relationships with each other, and with God. Jesus himself used slavery language to describe his own ministry and in his teaching on discipleship, and this influence is felt throughout the New Testament. The epistles provide evidence of communities trying to work out how masters and slaves should relate to each other and worship together, and their leaders' attempts to guide them.

Jesus and Slavery

Slaves feature regularly in Jesus' parables.[35] In some, they play incidental parts, as for example in the stories of the Great Banquet and the Weeds and the Wheat (Luke 14:16–24; Matt 13:24–30, 36–43). Those parables in which slaves have significant roles reflect the everyday reality of slavery in Roman Palestine.[36] The story of the Wicked Tenants draws on the fact that slaves could be subject to very cruel punishment from masters who could do whatever they wanted with them (Mark 12:1–11// Matt 21:33–44// Luke 20:9–18). As in the Parable of the Talents, some slaves were responsible for large sums of money or property (Matt 25:14–30). Thus, Jesus is appealing to everyday phenomena with which his hearers would be familiar. In the Parable of the Wicked Tenants, for example, slavery language is used to describe what happens when the gospel is rejected, and to press home the message that there is a responsibility to ensure that the community bears fruit.[37] The possibility of severe punishment, to which slaves were susceptible and accustomed, brought home the message of God's judgment.

But Jesus' use of the concept of slavery is much more than a storytelling device, it acts as a central metaphor to describe what it means to be his

---

35. *Doulos* has usually been translated as "servant" rather than "slave." See Harris, *Slave of Christ*, 183–91; Hultgren, *The Parables of Jesus*, 473–75. However, with the probable exception of the Parable of the Unjust Steward (Luke 16:1–8) in which the *doulos* is banished, rather than physically punished, "slave" is an appropriate translation (Glancy, *Slavery in Early Christianity*, 109). Since it is in the nature of the parable genre that hearers understand the stories according to their circumstances, the focus on slaves here should not be taken as suggesting that the parables cannot speak to those in servant rather than slave roles today. See Wright, *The Voice of Jesus*.

36. Schottroff, *The Parables of Jesus*, 171–87.

37. See Hultgren, *The Parables of Jesus*; Knowles, "Everyone Who Hears These Words of Mine."

disciple. Like good slaves, the disciples should be watchful (Mark 13:33–37; Luke 12:35–38), they should be faithful in everyday things, particularly in caring for and serving believers (Matt 24:45–51; Luke 12:42–46). They should do this with compassion and mercy (Matt 18:23–35) and in obedience to a gracious and generous God (Luke 17:7–10). All this is part of his teaching aimed at overturning the power structures of the world, both religious and political. The paradoxical nature of discipleship is that the truly great are those who become slaves (Mark 10:42–45; 9:33–37; Matt 20:26–28). In the kingdom of God, the servant is the one with authority.[38]

Slavery is not the only language used for discipleship. For example, in John 15:15 Jesus tells his disciples that they are no longer slaves but friends, on the same level as him, and that they know his business. Nevertheless, the emphasis on service is central to the response to Jesus as *kyrios*. And as service is the mark of the slave, the believers should not seek honor in the world. All this is exemplified in the life of Jesus, who describes himself as having come to serve and to give his life as a ransom for many (Mark 10:45). He is the slave who comes to proclaim release to the captives (Luke 4:16–19). He is both king and suffering servant.[39] The disciples, who are his slaves, must experience the same persecution and suffering as he does (Matt 10:25). However, in contrast to human masters who could be very cruel, Jesus the *kyrios'* yoke is easy (Matt 11:29–30).

Paul and Slavery

As the church grew, its teachers had to guide believers as they struggled to express these ideas in their lives. The Pauline communities consisted of people from different ranks in society who met together to worship Jesus as Messiah (e.g., 1 Cor 1:26; Phil 4:22).[40] But how were masters and slaves to understand themselves in the light of their allegiance to Christ? Two passages provide evidence of Paul's views on this question. In the letter to Philemon, Paul deals directly with the problem of a runaway slave named Onesimus. In 1 Corinthians 7 he briefly discusses the status of slaves in a passage primarily dealing with questions about marriage. Both have been

---

38. Santos, *Slave of All*; Carter, *Households and Discipleship*, 161–92.

39. Chisholm, "The Christological Fulfilment of Isaiah's Servant Songs."

40. See Meeks, *The First Urban Christians*, 21–22; 63–64. For an overview of scholarship on Paul and slavery see Byron, *Recent Research on Paul and Slavery*.

used to present a Paul who is concerned to maintain the social convention of slavery, but as we shall see, neither is straightforward.

Philemon

The letter to Philemon was appealed to by both sides of the American anti-slavery debate.[41] Pro-slavers understood Paul to be asking Philemon take Onesimus back; for abolitionists, he was seeking the slave's freedom. Today, there are several views of what might be going on in this short letter. One influential interpretation holds that Onesimus was not a runaway but had been sent by the church in Colossae to support Paul.[42] Another suggestion is that Onesimus is actually Philemon's brother and not a slave at all.[43] However, the traditional (and still majority) view is that Paul is asking Philemon to take his runaway slave back, without punishment, on the basis that he has become a brother in Christ.[44]

From an anti-slavery point of view we might wish that Paul had directly asked for Philemon to be freed. But he does not. Is he being deliberately obscure out of politeness to a social superior, not wishing to tell him what to do?[45] It seems that Paul wants Philemon to send Onesimus back to him (vv. 13–14), but it is unclear whether he has manumission in mind or not. The striking thing is that Paul speaks of Onesimus as Philemon's *brother*, and this means that he thinks of master and slave as equals. As Petersen notes, this line of argument strongly suggests that Paul is hinting at manumission.[46] Whether Philemon acted upon this implicit proposal, however, is unknown.

First Corinthians 7

Here, Paul is answering questions sent to him by the Corinthian church. Is marriage compatible with following of Christ? Should married people

41. Callahan, "The Letter to Philemon."

42. See Winter, "Paul's Letter to Philemon."

43. Callahan, *Embassy of Onesimus.*

44. Traditional readers of Philemon include Lohse, *Colossians and Philemon*; Barthe and Blanke, *The Letter to Philemon*; Nordling, "Onesimus Fugitivus."

45. Wilson, "The Pragmatics of Politeness and Pauline Epistolography."

46. Petersen, *Rediscovering Paul*; Lewis, "An African American Appraisal of the Philemon-Paul-Onesimus Triangle."

seek divorce? To these questions Paul has a general answer—remain as you are—don't divorce (and don't be celibate within marriage), and remain unmarried if you are single. The rule of thumb is that believers do not have to change their social status but should rather "retain the place in life that the Lord has assigned" to them. The same goes for Jewish men (who should not remove the marks of circumcision) and, it seems, for slaves. For in 7:21 Paul says, "Were you a slave when you were called? Do not be concerned about it." At first sight this suggests that slaves should not seek their freedom, but remain as they are. However, in the next sentence Paul qualifies the statement, and at this point the Greek becomes obscure, and is capable of two different interpretations.

According to the RSV, Paul goes on to say that if slaves can gain their freedom they should do so—"But if you can gain your freedom, avail yourself of the opportunity" (7:21). If this is the correct translation, Paul thinks that freedom is better than being enslaved. However, the Greek may also be translated as "make use of your present condition now more than ever" (NRSV).[47] In this case, Paul seems to say that they should make the most of their enslaved position for the sake of the gospel.

The second option would make sense in the light of our knowledge of the Greco-Roman world. Most slaves dreamt of freedom, but manumission did not remove all obligations to the owner. After paying a fee, the slave still had certain obligations outlined in a "staying agreement" (paramōne).[48] Under such circumstances it might have been more sensible for some to remain enslaved. However, the majority of interpreters opt for the first view.[49] One reason is that it is generally good practice in such "elliptical expressions" to supply a word from the immediate context, and "freedom" appears in verse 21a.[50] There is also a strong case to be made, on the basis of parallels with other Greek writings, that the pattern of his argument here suggests that slavery should be considered the exception to the rule.[51] Thus, slaves should seek freedom if possible, but this should not become the main focus of their lives—for the truth is that they are "free" in the sight of the

47. See Harrill, *Manumission*, 68–128.

48. Zelnick-Abramovitz, *Not Wholly Free*; De Vos "Once a Slave Always a Slave?"; Lyall, *Slaves, Citizens, Sons*.

49. But cf. Bartchy, ΜΑΛΛΟΝ ΧΡΕΣΑΙ, who argues that manumission was in the call of the owner, not the slave.

50. Ciampa and Rosner, *The First Letter to the Corinthians*, 316–27.

51. For a summary of the arguments for this view see Garland, *1 Corinthians*, 298–316.

Lord. Spiritually speaking, social status becomes a matter of indifference for the believer, for it is one's relationship to Christ that constitutes one's identity. All believers, whether master or slave, are slaves of Christ, and they should not become "enslaved" to maintaining their rank in society, for there is, ultimately, no difference between freedmen and slaves in the church community (7:22).

Slavery as metaphor in Paul

Like Jesus, Paul uses slave metaphors to teach his congregations about the nature of discipleship.[52] His self-designation as a "slave of Christ" or of God (Rom 1:1; Gal 1:10; 2 Cor 6:2–4) may suggest that he identifies himself with prophets such as Jeremiah and Isaiah who saw themselves as slaves of Yahweh (Isa 49:3; Jer 7:25).[53] If this is the case, he is claiming a certain authority—his words should be heard. Alongside this however, he also says that *all* believers are "slaves of Christ" (1 Cor 7:22; Rom 14:18), regardless of social status. Their *kyrios* is the paradigmatic slave of God (Phil 2:7), whose coming into the world inverts all social hierarchies, and their response should be one of service to each other.[54] Thus Paul can also describe himself as the slave of believers, for he serves them by preaching Christ (2 Cor 4:5).

Certainly, different social groupings would have heard Paul's use of slavery language differently, depending on their own position in life. As Castelli points out, if Paul's readers associated slavery with brutality then the idea of being a slave of Christ and serving other believers may not always have been seen as positive.[55] However, Paul's use of the slavery metaphor must be seen in relation to the overarching message of the gospel: freedom in Christ. Believers are "slaves of Christ," but they are, paradoxically, free. They have been released from slavery to sin (Rom 8:2) and from the elemental spirits of the universe, which held people in thrall until Christ came (Gal 4:3). Crucially too, slavery imagery needs to be seen alongside

52. Combes, *The Metaphor of Slavery in the Writings of the Early Church*, 91.

53. On 2 Cor 6:2 see Gignilliat, *Paul and Isaiah's Servants*. On Gal 1:10 see Dodd, "Christ's Slave, People Pleasers and Galatians 1:10."

54. Briggs, "Can an Enslaved God Liberate?" Schrage, *The Ethics of the New Testament*, 232–35.

55. Castelli, "Romans," 294. Cf. however Dale B. Martin's argument in *Slavery as Salvation* that conversion could have been seen as "upward mobility" for slaves.

that of kinship. In baptism, all believers are transferred from one sphere of being to an other, they are now "in Christ" (Rom 6:1–20). This implied spiritual equality has its strongest expression in a baptismal formula which declares that "There is no longer Jew or Greek, there is no longer slave or free, there is no longer male and female; for all of you are one in Christ Jesus" (Gal 3:28; cf. 1 Cor 12:13; Col 3:11).

The norms of the world are now invalid in the church—what matters is not earthly status or role, but one's relationship to Christ. However, it is highly unlikely that the ideal encapsulated in this formula was ever put into practice.[56] Indeed, it would have been very difficult to do so. Since house-groups met in private homes, social differences would be very obvious each time the community met, and tensions would inevitably surface.[57] But to focus on the actual eradication of the dichotomies is to miss the point. Slavery is included, alongside categories of race and gender, because people would relate to it. Paul cites the formula to help believers understand their identity as brothers and sisters "in Christ." He is no more concerned to abolish slavery than he is to eradicate the difference between men and women. What is important to him is unity amongst believers; he does not want the church to be compromised by squabbles about status and social difference.

We cannot say that Paul was arguing against slavery or trying to give a "generally valid rule."[58] However, he does indirectly question the place of slavery in society. In Philemon, his use of family language challenges the usual view of the relationship between slaves and masters. In 1 Corinthians, his view that the social distinction between master and slave is of no spiritual significance is striking in a world in which one's social status assumes high importance. In an honor-driven society, his use of the slavery metaphor underscores his teaching that for disciples of Jesus, honor is to be found in quite a different way from the world outside.[59]

---

56. *Pace* Fiorenza, "The Praxis of Co-Equal Discipleship."

57. Barclay, "Paul, Philemon and the Dilemma of Christian Slave-Ownership."

58. Lohse, *Colossians and Philemon*, 188.

59. See deSilva, *Honor, Patronage, Kinship and Purity.* On honor and shame see Pilch and Malina, *Handbook of Biblical Social Values,* 106–7; Brown, "Paul's Use of ΔΟΥΛΟΣ ΧΡΙΣΤΟΥ ΙΗΣΟΥ."

The *Haustafeln*

Thus far we have observed an emphasis on freedom as a fundamental value for Christians, and a concomitant subversion of social norms within the church. Disciples are made free to serve others, and in the church community the hierarchies that characterize the world are undermined, even reversed. Because of the work and example of Christ, the weak become strong. Christian values are the opposite of those found in society. This might encourage us to see an implicit anti-slavery trend in the New Testament. However, some passages seem to work against this view. In Ephesians, Colossians, 1 Peter, and in the Pastoral epistles, slaves are exhorted to be obedient to their masters. For slaveholders in antebellum America, these passages provided proof of the divine approval of slavery. For example, 1 Timothy 6:1–2 seemed to provide exactly what slaves needed to hear:

> Let all who are under the yoke of slavery regard their masters as
> worthy of all honor, so that the name of God and the teaching may
> not be blasphemed. Those who have believing masters must not be
> disrespectful on the ground that they are members of the church;
> rather they must serve them all the more since those who benefit
> by their service are believers and beloved.

Slave owners viewed these passages in much the same way as they viewed Old Testament law—as timeless prescriptions to be obeyed without question. Slaves were to see service to their earthly masters as service to God himself, who would reward them in the world to come. It comes as no surprise to learn that black theologians today consider the *Haustafeln* to have exerted "a malefic and far reaching impact on the lives of African Americans."[60] So what should we do with them? We have seen that the Hebrew legal collections should not be taken as blanket rules for all time, but as contingent to their time and circumstances. The same applies to the *Haustafeln*. Like the Old Testament lawmakers, the writers of these epistles desired to see order in the community.

In the Colossians and Ephesians *Haustafeln* (Eph 6:5–9 is probably an expanded version of Col 3:22—4:1), slaves are urged to be obedient to their masters, regarding their hard work as service to God.

> Slaves, obey your earthly masters in everything, not only while
> being watched and in order to please them, but wholeheartedly

60. C. J. Martin, "The Haustafeln (Household Codes) in African American Biblical Interpretation," 206. See further Meeks, "The 'Haustafeln' and American Slavery."

fearing the Lord. Whatever your task, put yourselves into it, as done for the Lord and not for your masters, since you know that from the Lord you will receive the inheritance as your reward; you serve the Lord Jesus Christ. For the wrongdoer will be paid back for whatever wrong has been done, and there is no partiality. Masters, treat your slaves justly and fairly, for you know that you also have a Master in heaven. (Col 3:22—4:1)

At first sight these instructions seem to be deeply conformist, and in fact, similar advice is found in non-Christian sources of the time. However, three features make them distinctive. First (in contrast to comparable lists of instructions found in the Greco-Roman world), the author addresses slaves directly—as human beings. Second, obedience is required, not in order to gain their masters' favor, but because they are slaves of Christ, from whom they will receive their reward. Their owners are merely their earthly masters. Third, masters are also described as slaves of Christ—they too will be answerable to him. Lastly, in Ephesians, all this appears under the rubric of an instruction that they should all be subject to one another (5:21). Instead of mutual suspicion, slaves and masters must treat each other with respect.[61] They should see each other as brothers and sisters who all have the same father (Eph 1:2, 5; Col 1:2).[62]

A similar balancing of spiritual equality with social reality occurs in 1 Peter. Wishing to encourage in times of persecution, he tells his readers that they are both a "royal priesthood" (2:9) and "servants of God" (2:16).[63] With this in mind, Christian *oiketai* (household slaves) of non-believing masters should be respectful, even of those who ill-treat them. As Christ himself endured injustice, so should they, without seeking redress. The idea of conformity to Christ in suffering is intended to comfort slaves and encourage them in a life in which there was unavoidable unjust suffering.[64] They have a good shepherd and guardian for their souls (2:25).

The writers of Colossians, Ephesians, and 1 Peter continue in the Pauline vein of subtly undermining social norms. Slavery may be the societal norm, but spiritually speaking, all believers are equal. In the Pastoral Epistles, however, any such egalitarian undercurrent seems to be absent.

61. Gombis, "A Radical New Humanity."

62. See Aasgaard, "'Brotherly Advice.'"

63. See Sandnes, "Revised Conventions in Early Christian Parenesis."

64. Elliott, *A Home for the Homeless*, 128ff; Balch, *Let Wives Be Submissive*, 119; Osiek and Balch, *Families in the New Testament World*, 190.

Kinship language and the Christological motivation for service is lacking—masters are not addressed and slaves are simply instructed to "toe the line."

There may be several reasons for this. Numerous scholars suggest that the Pastoral Epistles reflect a time when the church is becoming institutionalized after the death of Paul.[65] It may be that the writer assumes that his readers already know the underlying theology and does not feel the need to repeat it.[66] Or it may be that, in the face of persecution, leaders sense a need to conform to the hierarchical structure of the surrounding culture for the sake of furthering the gospel.[67] Thinking of themselves as being in the end times, anything distinguishing them from the outside world must be underplayed, including the subversive idea that slaves and free could be equal.[68]

The New Testament and Slavery: Wider Aspects

Since one-third of Greco-Roman society was made up of slaves, it is natural that slaves and slavery imagery should play a large part in the New Testament writings.[69] Slaves feature in the stories of the first believers (for example, Rhoda in Acts 12:13–15, and the healing of the centurion's slave girl in Matt 8:5–13; Luke 7:1–10) and of Peter's denial of Jesus in Matt 26:69–75 (cf. Mark 14:66–72; Luke 22:54–62; John 18:15–18). Further, slavery metaphors are found throughout the New Testament. Men and women are described as slaves to sin (John 8:34; Rom 6:16–20; Gal 5:1), to alcohol (Titus 2:3), or to the fear of death (Heb 2:15).[70] The idea that believers are slaves of God (e.g., Jas 1:1; Acts 2:18; 4:29; 1 Pet 2:16; Rev 7:3; 19:2,5), just as Israel is the slave of Yahweh (e.g., Isa 41:8–10; 65:13–14), is found throughout the New Testament.[71] In Revelation, the slaves of God (Rev 1:6) will spend eternity worshipping God and the lamb (Rev 22:3).

The exodus story plays a significant role. Matthew's Gospel sees the return of Jesus and his family from Egypt as fulfilling Hosea 11:1—"out of

65. MacDonald, *The Pauline Churches*; Aageson, *Paul, the Pastoral Epistles and the Early Church*; Hays, *Moral Vision*, 66–72; Verner, *The Household of God*, 140–45.

66. See, e.g., Hays, *Moral Vision*, 71.

67. Knight, *The Pastoral Epistles*, 245–46.

68. Kidd, *Wealth and Beneficence in the Pastoral Epistles*.

69. Rollins, "Slavery in the NT," 832.

70. Harris, *Slave of Christ*, 52.

71. See Byron, *Slavery Metaphors*.

Egypt I have called my son" (Matt 2:15). Jesus, the second Moses, leads his people from captivity to sin into freedom of serving others.[72] Paul's self-designation as a slave of Christ indicates that he associates himself with the history of Israel and the foundational story of exodus and covenant.[73] In the Apocalypse, the exodus underlies John's thinking with regard to God's work of redemption, judgment, and inheritance, and it will soon be enacted for the final time (22:6). Liberation from the political powers is seen as analogous to the exodus.[74]

Two passages refer to the slave trade in derogatory fashion—1 Timothy 1:9–10 and Revelation 18:13. In 1 Timothy, in the course of a polemic against false teachers, the author lists those who may be considered "lawless and disobedient." Included in that list, amongst murderers, the sexually immoral, and liars, are slave-traders (*andropodistais*). It is unlikely that this should be seen as a direct protest against the slave trade itself, for the writer is primarily concerned to undermine his opponents, and the list is merely a rhetorical device to make his point.[75] Nevertheless, the behavior of slave-traders, who were notorious for kidnapping ordinary people and dishonest dealings, is denounced as an extreme example of stealing, and contrary to the message of the gospel.[76]

The writer of the Apocalypse is similarly not concerned to stop the slave trade. He is, rather, protesting against the greed and corruption of the Roman Empire. However, in the course of his attack, we find the nearest thing to a critique of the slave trade to be found in the New Testament. When, in his vision, Babylon meets her downfall, those merchants who have made their fortunes under her regime find that their trade is ended, there being no demand for their merchandise. John's list of their goods, which are mostly luxury, ends with the "bodies and souls of men," in other words, slaves (18:13). The use of this phrase, which emphasizes the fact that some of the goods are actually human beings, along with the rhetorical impact of its place as last in the list, suggests that he thinks the slave trade

---

72. Ibid., 260; Allison, *The New Moses*; Lierman, *The New Testament Moses*.

73. Byron, *Slavery Metaphors*, 58; Keesmaat, *Paul and His Story*.

74. Fiorenza, "Redemption as Liberation"; Casey, "The Exodus Theme in the Book of Revelation."

75. McEleney, "The Vice Lists of the Pastoral Epistles"; Marshall, *A Critical Commentary on the Pastoral Epistles*, 380.

76. Harrill, "The Vice of Slave Dealers in Greco-Roman Society."

is an iniquitous element in the greed of the Roman Empire, in whose ethos and behavior believers should play no part (18:4).[77]

Conclusion on the New Testament and Slavery

Slaves feature strongly in the New Testament, both actually and metaphorically. The central paradox of the Son of God who took the form of a slave is to be imitated by believers who, as slaves of Christ (and therefore God), have been set free for obedience to God.[78] At times, this freedom is spoken of as an ideal—in Christ there should be no division between slave and free (Gal 3:28). Most often, however, the tension between this and social reality has to be maintained.

The exodus narrative has a strong influence. For the Gospel writers, especially Matthew, Jesus is the new Moses. According to Paul, Jesus will lead Israel to freedom once again (Rom 11:26; cf. Isa 59:20–21). Particularly in Revelation, there is an echo of the prophetic call of the Old Testament against abusive power structures that create poverty, corruption, and greed, and that ultimately enslave the poor. Nevertheless, slavery itself is not attacked explicitly, nor is it seen as a moral problem. To understand this lack of overt challenge to slavery as an institution, we need to remember that to speak of its abolition would have been to try to overturn religious, economic, and political structures—something with which they are not concerned, and which would only have brought about social chaos.[79] As Richard Horsley says, "The only way of imagining a society without slavery would have been to imagine a different society."[80] Thus, we find the epistle writers wrestling with the implications of this message for the nascent church. Within the community those who are non-persons in the outside world are full members of the church—all are brothers and sisters in Christ. While the writer(s) of Colossians and Ephesians may have been able to maintain some tension between social reality and the equalizing tendencies of the gospel, those of the pastorals seem unable to do so, perhaps because of the pressure to accommodate to the surrounding Greco-Roman society.[81]

77. Koester, "Roman Slave Trade and the Critique of Babylon."

78. Carter, *The Servant-Ethic in the New Testament.*

79. Harris, *Slave of Christ*, 67.

80. Horsley, "The Slave Systems of Classical Antiquity," 58.

81. See Lampe, "The Language of Equality in Early Christian House Churches."

4. CONCLUSION

What then, if anything, can the Bible contribute to a Christian response to contemporary human trafficking? The difference between our worldview and that of the Bible could tempt us into thinking that it can have nothing to say on the matter. However, this view fails to do justice to the nature of the Bible. By adopting a canonical approach to Scripture we have tried to flesh out what a biblically informed view of human trafficking might look like. While it is true that slavery is never denounced or prohibited, the overarching message of Scripture is one of redemption. Its central values of freedom, justice, and human dignity are expressed in many different ways.[82] In the Old Testament, it is found pre-eminently in the collective memory of liberation preserved in the account of the exodus, but also in other narratives, and prophecy and wisdom literature, which undermine and subvert society's ideas as to who has power and status and who does not. For all these writers, slavery is felt to be at odds with the inherent dignity of humanity, and the complacency of those who accept the prevailing world order because it suits their purposes is constantly challenged. This "redemptive impulse" reaches its fulfillment in the New Testament salvation drama.[83] Jesus comes to redeem the world and to set the captives free, and teaches that the values of God's kingdom are the opposite of the power, wealth, and status, which are important to the world. Those with least honor in society, including slaves, are actually first in God's sight. Christ, the slave-king comes to serve those without power and status in society, and he demands that his followers, his "slaves" do the same. If this is what Jesus' followers are called to do, it follows that there is a moral imperative for Christians to see slavery and the exploitation of others as incompatible with all that we know and understand of the love of God. To work against human trafficking must therefore be central to the church's work of embodying God's love in the world.

The canonical approach adopted here, with its Christological focus and the ethic that flows from it, reminds us of the theological basis for anti-trafficking work. It also helps us to answer the question with regard to the place of those passages that seem to be at odds with the "law of love." As we have seen, several strands of tradition are represented in the texts that make

82. Wright, "Response to Gordon McConville."

83. Cf. Webb, *Slaves, Women and Homosexuals*, who speaks of a "redemptive spirit." See further Birch, *Let Justice Roll Down*, 132; Ringe, *Jesus, Liberation, and the Biblical Jubilee.*

up the canon of Scripture. Not only do we have the "redemptive impulse" and its fulfillment in Jesus Christ, we also have recorded the voices of those who, like us, have an imperfect understanding of how to respond to it while, at the same time, living in a world that demands that it conform to cultural expectations and norms. The legal texts and paraenetic instruction in the epistles represent the attempts to provide stability and community order as the Hebrews and early Christians struggled to live out their understanding of what it means to be the people of God in a sometimes hostile world.

Understanding of the place of biblical law and paraenesis in this way should help us to avoid the pitfalls that so hindered the Princetonians, who sensed that slavery was incompatible with the will of God but were hidebound by a need for direct prescription and to follow what they understood to be God's law applicable in every age. Instead, we see that the abolitionists' focus on God's love for his people and the need to eradicate injustice, rather than on prescription and law, remains valid as a hermeneutical basis on which to read Scripture for moral and social change. It remains true that the law of love encapsulates all moral requirements, and that all other laws and instructions must be measured against it. And it remains true that the Bible's central message of God's redeeming love for his world not only demands that slavery must be seen as incompatible with that message but that those who profess to be disciples of Christ must declare it to be so.

A biblically informed anti-slavery stance, however, entails much more than the mere condemnation of human trafficking. As the redeemed people of God, Christians are no longer in thrall to the ambitions and power-struggles of the world in which we live. We are free to work for the justice, dignity, and freedom that are at the heart of the canonical vision for God's people, and to answer the call to identify with the most vulnerable in society. So too, we are free to refuse to collude in or be a part of systems that abuse and exploit the vulnerable, and to speak out for those who are silenced by oppression. As the Old Testament prophets remind us, this requires working against the poverty that drives people into slavery and speaking out against the greed and corruption that motivates and perpetuates the trade in human beings. It also requires a re-examination of our own attitudes towards money. Jesus may not have spoken out against slavery, but he did have plenty to say on the subject of wealth and possessions (e.g., Matt 6:19–34; Mark 10:17–25), as the early church understood (Acts 2:43–45; 1 Tim 6:10; Heb 13:5). Further, we can care for those who have been damaged by slavery, and actively support those who make it their business to seek out and rescue the enslaved. At the same time, we can proclaim that those who oppress, exploit, and enslave others are not only harming others, but compromising their own human dignity. The imperative of Scripture is unavoidable, and there is much to do. There can be no room for complacency in the church on this matter. For, the existence of slavery is an affront to all that Christianity represents—the redeeming God who sets the captives free.

CHAPTER 4

The Problem of Prostitution

1. INTRODUCTION

In every age, slavery appears in different forms. The slavery that the nineteenth-century abolitionists tackled was different from that of the ancient Greco-Roman world, which in turn was different from the slavery of the Old Testament era. Similarly, changing ideologies, power structures, and economies mean that the reasons for slavery differ from age to age and even from culture to culture. What remains constant, however, is that men and women are forced to work under coercion and without the freedom to leave, and are viewed as commodities and property, rather than as human beings.

Thus far I have been considering slavery as a whole—in all its many forms. In this section I wish to narrow the focus down to one particular form of modern-day slavery—sex trafficking. Why is this necessary? Slavery, sexual exploitation, and prostitution have always been closely linked.[1] There are many accounts of sexual abuse of slaves by their masters, and the sale of human beings to be used as prostitutes is nothing new.[2] Why is this a particular area of concern for a Christian response to human trafficking?

1. Bullough and Bullough, *Prostitution*, 21; Brooten, "Introduction" in Brooten, *Beyond Slavery*, 1–29.

2. For example, the Victorian feminist writer Harriet Martineau, in her travel record *Society in America*, compared the Southern plantations to eastern harems, and criticized

There are two main reasons. Firstly, there is a problem of attitudes to prostitution. In theory, there should be no difference between our response to the family that finds itself in debt-bondage to a quarry owner, and the woman who finds herself enslaved in a brothel. Both may have been destitute, both may have been coerced or tricked into their current situation, both may be unable to leave for fear of violence. However, victims of sex trafficking can find themselves facing particular problems in addition to enslavement. Subjected to repeated rape and physical and sexual abuse, they are left with enduring and profound psychological and physical trauma. Those who are forced to work in prostitution face an additional burden, for in many cultures, they become not only "socially dead" slaves, but "whores," stigmatized outsiders who have broken social norms.[3] Such deep-seated cultural, social, and religious responses to those involved in prostitution (whether voluntarily or involuntarily) can compromise the response to sex trafficking at every level—from the enforcement of legislation to care of victims. For many Christians, this inhibits willingness to become involved in aid and rescue work for victims of sex trafficking. Conversely, and perhaps in reaction to this, some become so concerned about the suffering victims that other forms of slavery are neglected.[4] Second, there is today considerable debate with regard to how the sex trade should be viewed, and this has a direct bearing on discussions as to how sex trafficking should be tackled. Would, for example, abolishing the sex trade reduce the numbers trafficked into prostitution? Or should we be making the sex trade a legitimate enterprise, subject to taxation and employment law, thus taking the stigma and criminality out of it? It is important that Christians understand these and other arguments in order to be able to contribute to the discussion in an informed manner.

In this chapter, I propose to open up the topic of prostitution, demonstrating its complexity, and inviting readers to examine their own attitudes to the sex trade. Taking it as read that all sexual activity between adults and children is by its very nature abusive and exploitative, I will restrict

the licentiousness of the owners who wanted to populate their plantations with unpaid workers. See Logan, *Fallenness In Victorian Women's Writing*, 159–88; Clinton, "Breaking the Silence"; Burnard, *Mastery, Tyranny and Desire*; Walvin, *The Trader, the Owner, the Slave*, 105–75.

3. The phrase is Orlando Patterson's; see his *Slavery and Social Death*. While it is true that attitudes to prostitutes can vary from culture to culture, as Laurie Schrage points out (*Moral Dilemmas of Feminism*, 99–119), stigma against them is common.

4. See for example, Zimmermann, *Other Dreams of Freedom*.

our discussion to adult prostitution, which the *Oxford English Dictionary* defines as "engaging in sexual activity with someone for payment."[5] As an introduction to the subject, we will consider a short story by the French writer Guy de Maupassant that skillfully captures the ambivalence that tends to characterize reactions to prostitutes and prostitution. We will then outline the history of the church's response to prostitution, and introduce current discussions regarding the sex trade. The aim is not only to inform Christians about prostitution and its relation to sex trafficking, but also to set the hermeneutical context for a study of what the Bible might have to say on the matter.

2. BUTTERBALL

Boule de Suif (or *Butterball* in the English translation) was published in France in 1880 as part of a collection of "naturalist" writings on the subject of the Franco-Prussian war.[6] In it, Maupassant set out to suggest that the hypocrisy of the bourgeoisie was responsible for the defeat of France.[7] The idea of the prostitute is a metaphor for the view that France had prostituted herself before the enemy. The story is not therefore about prostitution as such, but about the war; however, it skillfully exposes and explores attitudes and responses to it.

The story concerns ten people who hire a coach in order to leave the French town of Rouen, which has been taken over by German soldiers.[8] Bound for Le Havre, the group is made up of three married couples, two nuns, a single man, and "Butterball," who is so called because she is short, round, and fat. Two of the married men are businessmen—one respectable, the other not quite so scrupulous. The third couple are titled nobility, with possible (though morally questionable) familial links to royalty. The

5. This is not to deny that child prostitution is a major part of contemporary sex trafficking. The restriction is solely for the purposes of a discussion of the morality of prostitution.

6. The collection of stories was called *Les Soirées de Médan* (1888). On naturalism see Furst and Skrine *Naturalism* (on Maupassant see especially 27–28). Naturalist writers aimed to describe human behavior in scientific detail. Maupassant's adherence to the ideal, however, was incomplete, "for he was never able to subscribe wholeheartedly to the scientific pretensions to the representation of man in society which that view entailed." (Chaplin, *Maupassant*, 19.)

7. Chaplin, *Boule de Suif*, 53.

8. Maupassant, *Butterball*.

single male traveller, Cornudet, has a reputation for "democratic" politics and drinking too much.

The married ladies immediately look down on Butterball. The nuns have nothing to do with anyone, busily saying their prayers. The men talk business. Due to heavy snow the journey takes much longer than expected, and the passengers become very hungry. Butterball, who is the only one who has had the foresight to bring any food, is generous in sharing the contents of her hamper. The initial disdain towards her lessens as all the passengers, including the nuns, enjoy the food and wine. The coach arrives at the town of Tôtes, where they will spend the night. However, a problem arises when the Prussian officer who is presiding over the town demands that Butterball sleep with him. Outraged, Butterball refuses, on the grounds that he is the enemy. At first the ladies (the nuns are seldom seen, escaping the group to be with the local priest) support her, but when it becomes evident that they will not be allowed to leave Tôtes until she complies, and hours become days, their sympathy evaporates. What is sleeping with a German to her? She sleeps with anyone, so why not him? Talking about her in her absence, they refer to her as a "hussy," a "slut," a "whore."

Thus, as long as their journey cannot be resumed, her refusal to sleep with the officer becomes morally reprehensible. The nuns add their voice. "Nothing," declares one, "could fail to be pleasing to the Lord when the intention behind it is praiseworthy," and she implies that in failing to grant the officer his wish Butterball is indirectly contributing to the deaths of French soldiers whom they are going to Le Havre to nurse. Finally, the Count tries to cajole Butterball into doing the "act of kindness" which is part and parcel of her profession.

Eventually, Butterball capitulates, much against her will, and the group (which celebrates with a rather bawdy party) is allowed to leave the next day. However, now that they have got what they wanted, the "respectable" passengers, who previously shared her food and wine, will have nothing to do with her. In fact, they move away from her as if she were impure, and do not share with her the food they have brought with them. Butterball weeps for the rest of the journey and only Cornudet expresses disgust at the behavior of his fellow travellers.

In the second half of the nineteenth century, French writers and artists were preoccupied with the idea of prostitution and the threat it might pose to society as a whole. Following a study by J. B. Parent-Duchâtelet in the 1830s, prostitution had been regulated with a view to protecting

French society from moral and physical disease.[9] Duchâtelet's work fascinated writers and artists of the period because of the picture he painted of the type of women who became prostitutes. They invariably came from backgrounds of poverty, and were, he said, inclined towards libertinism, laziness, and the pursuit of pleasure. This meant that they easily fell into the trap of prostitution, and even worse, the dreadful disease of lesbianism. The prostitute, then, represented everything that was disorderly and unstable, and her degeneracy could easily seep into decent society.[10]

Maupassant, like his friend and mentor Gustave Flaubert, frequented brothels himself and despised what he saw as the hypocrisy and double standards of the bourgeoisie. His disdain of "respectability" shows itself in his depiction of the passengers, who are hypocritical and shallow. They will take from Butterball and be friendly towards her when it suits them, but they are really interested only in their own concerns. She is expendable, and is rejected after she does what they want. They are therefore no better than the Prussian soldier. Her tears as she leaves Tôtes are ascribed to "shame," but her companions have been fascinated, titillated, and even made jealous (in the case of one of the ladies) by the thought of her sleeping with the German.

Butterball becomes a scapegoat, to be cast aside and punished as a threat to the stability of her fellow passengers' lives. She is also the whore who seems to stand in sharp contrast with the supposed purity of the nuns. But she is also necessary. She takes away the effluent of the Prussian officer's lust, and so protects reputable society from harm. She serves a purpose— but as the vessel for that lust she is impure, and the fellow passengers run the risk of contamination—hence, when she has done the deed, they turn away from her.

But Butterball does have moral principles. She is staunchly patriotic and has her own standards as to whom she will sleep with. She is, in her own way, much more moral than the men in the story who can ogle her and proposition her with impunity. She is also generous and thoughtful, and turns out to be more honest and transparent than the others, whose scruples about her sexual behavior conveniently disappear when they see that she can be useful to them. Moreover, Butterball herself shows far more

---

9. Parent-Duchâtelet, *De la Prostitution dans la Ville de Paris*. See further Bernheimer, *Figures of Ill Repute*, 8–33.

10. See Corbin, *Women for Hire*, 3–29.

humanity and honor than any of the others, ultimately sacrificing herself for her compatriots.

Boule de Suif was highly successful in its time, even considered to be the best in the group of stories. It may not have been as rigorously "naturalist" and objective as the Médan group would have liked, but Maupassant captures the complexities and ambiguities with regard to prostitution, which characterize not only his age, but every age.[11] For, as we shall see, the question of prostitution is always bound up with notions of purity and impurity, of honor and shame, of the sacred and profane. Moreover, Maupassant points out that these dualities, which seem to exclude the prostitute from respectable society, are inevitably compromised by the fact that human beings are much more complex than they allow, and that the notion of the prostitute as the personification of all evil might not be as simple as it at first appears. For wherever sexuality plays a part, human relations become less than straightforward.

3. ATTITUDES TO PROSTITUTION IN HISTORICAL PERSPECTIVE

In the eyes of many Christians today, the best way to deal with prostitution is to eradicate it. However, the church has not always taken this view. For both Augustine and Thomas Aquinas, prostitution was a "necessary evil." In Augustine's opinion, to try to get rid of prostitution would be to court trouble. "Remove the prostitutes from human affairs," he said, "and you will unsettle everything on account of lusts."[12] For Thomas Aquinas, prostitution was to be equated with a sewer, which kept society clean—unpleasant, but necessary.[13] In medieval Europe, the church was so concerned with discouraging sodomy that it ran its own brothels for its armies and priests.[14] Prostitution was an essential means of keeping the troops and the priesthood happy, and under control.

11. See O'Neill, *Prostitution and Feminism*, 136.

12. Augustine, *De Ordine* II.4 (12) quoted in Rossiaud, *Medieval Prostitution*, 80, (discussion in pages 80–85). On medieval prostitution see further Karras, *Common Women*.

13. *Summa Theologica*, 2–2.153.2.

14. Histories of prostitution include Bullough and Bullough, *Prostitution*; Scott, *The History of Prostitution*; Ringdal, *Love for Sale*. See also Naphy, *Sex Crimes*, 61–80.

However, from early on, the church's response was characterized by double standards. While some holy men may have been able to control their sexual urges and live chaste lives, it was deemed natural (if distasteful) that most men's sexual urges needed to have an outlet—both for the sake of their health and social order. Always, however, the idea was that women were to blame for these urges in the first place. In fact, women in general (not simply prostitutes) were seen as a source of sin. Clement thought that every woman should think shame on herself for having been born female, and Tertullian declared women to be the cause of all sin in the world.[15] Early on, too, stories were told of repentant prostitutes who became exemplary monastics having renounced a life of sin.[16] In these narratives, the harlots are said to have been dissolute sinners, because of unrestrained desire (whether for physical or monetary gratification), and to have lived lives of ascetic penitence in the wilderness following conversion. Perfection could be brought about by personal renunciation, in obedience to the gospel and in imitation of Christ.

An increasing emphasis on chastity as a prerequisite for holiness did nothing for a healthy view of women.[17] They became a "moral danger," excluded from church roles. Women's holiness required virginity, and the giving up of their sexuality as pure brides of Christ.[18] During the medieval period the cult of the Virgin grew alongside the idea that sexuality and marriage were the result of the fall. Thus, the idea of virginity as the epitome of moral cleanliness developed. The Virgin's opposite was Mary Magdalene, the model for repentant whores.[19] Given such a culture, it is hardly surprising that prostitutes came to exemplify all that was wicked. Prostitutes themselves, were considered to be on the same level as Jewry—unclean, inevitable, essential.[20] Generally speaking, they had no legal rights, were expected to repent and convert, and live a life of purity.

15. See Ruether, *New Woman, New Earth*, 3–35.

16. See Ward, *Harlots of the Desert*; Brock & Harvey, *Holy Women of the Syrian Orient*.

17. See Brown, *The Body and Society*; Ranke-Heinemann, *Eunuchs for the Kingdom of Heaven*; Meeks, *The Origins of Christian Morality*, 130–49.

18. Castelli, "Virginity and Its Meaning for Women's Sexuality"; Rouselle, *Porneia*.

19. On the growth of the cult of the Virgin Mary see Pelikan, *Mary through the Centuries*; see further Schaberg, *The Resurrection of Mary Magdalene*; De Boer, *The Mary Magdalene Cover-Up*; Haskins, *Mary Magdalene*.

20. On medieval prostitution see further Karras, *Common Women*; Otis, *Prostitution in Medieval Society*.

Attitudes changed during the Reformation. Both Luther and Calvin considered marriage to be the appropriate context in which sexual and emotional needs were to be met, and brothels were closed down. But even in Calvin's Geneva, prostitution could not be eradicated. Thereafter, throughout Europe, the focus was on trying to keep prostitution away from respectable society, and efforts began to be made to reform the women who were responsible. In the eighteenth century, asylums were opened to house and reform "penitents." But the concept of "fallen women" was fluid, and could be applied to any woman or girl who had been seduced or raped. The earliest of the Dublin "Magdalen Asylums," as they were known, was opened in 1767, promising women that they would be sheltered from "Shame, from Reproach, from Disease, from Want, from the base Society that has either drawn you into vice, or prevailed upon you to continue in it, to the utmost hazard of your eternal happiness."[21] Girls were set to work in laundries in harsh regimes, given religious instruction, and kept out of the public view. Certainly, there was a growing awareness that prostitutes often suffered greatly, as a number of novels show, but the idea persisted that it was the women who should repent and purge themselves of their sin rather than their male customers.[22]

By the time Maupassant was writing, syphilis had become a major problem, and moral standards were considered to be low. Duchâtelet, whose idea of *réglementation* was influential throughout Europe, had made his name by conducting a study of the sewerage system in Paris, considered prostitutes to be the sewers of morality, draining away the excess passions of young men who would otherwise bring them into respectable society, with detrimental effect. The filth had to be removed, but the system of removal—the women—was necessary, their activities regulated in strictly policed *maisons de tolérance*.

---

21. Luddy, *Prostitution and Irish Society*, 77. See further Lewis and Ellis, *Prostitution and Eighteenth-Century Culture*. On the Magdalen laundries see Bartley, *Prostitution*; Mahood, *The Magdalenes*. On British evangelical institutions, see Shaw, *High Calvinists in Action*, 94–98; Heasman, *Evangelicals in Action*, 148–68.

22. Barbara Montegu's fictional *The Histories of Some of the Penitents of the Magdalen-House* (1760) was written to advertise the work of the Magdalen Charity in London Hospital. Famous nineteenth-century examples include Mrs. Gaskell's novel *Ruth Barton*, Nancy in Dickens' *Oliver Twist*, and Dostoevsky's Sonja in *Crime and Punishment*. See Ellis, *The Politics of Sensibility*, 160–89.

In Britain, studies analyzed the "Great Social Evil."[23] The high level of venereal disease amongst soldiers was believed to be caused by prostitution, and the Contagious Diseases Acts (1864, 1866, 1869) were introduced to combat it. But the attempt to supply the military with disease-free women met with strong opposition. Josephine Butler, who campaigned vigorously against the laws, successfully argued that they not only sanctioned state licensed slavery, but also revealed double standards: women were to be examined against their will while the behavior of men went unquestioned. As in Maupassant's story, men were able to act with impunity, while transgressing women became the scapegoat. The acts were eventually repealed, and a system of "repression and rescue" became the norm in Britain.[24]

Attempts to regulate prostitution were rigorously opposed by the early feminist, Josephine Butler, who protested against the double standards in the legislation.[25] However, her campaign was not universally appreciated. When she suggested that men who frequented prostitutes should be targeted for health checks she was met with threats and insults.[26] In an age when women were expected to stay out of the public sphere, her efforts to bring the European traffic in young girls to the attention of the general public were met with hostility—to the extent that she was called a "whore" herself.[27]

In late nineteenth-century Britain and America, feminists continued to be unanimously opposed to prostitution, but there were two schools of thought as to how to tackle it. On the one hand, there were "social purity feminists" who wanted to see prostitutes removed from entertainment venues, the brothels closed, and the streets cleared. They wanted to help

23. Acton, *Prostitution, Considered in Its Moral, Social and Sanitary Aspects*; see also Mayhew and Hemyng, *London Labour and the London Poor*; Sanger, *History of Prostitution*.

24. See Lee, *Policing Prostitution*; Fisher, *Prostitution and the Victorians*; McHugh, *Prostitution and Victorian Social Reform*; Bristow, *Vice and Vigilance*. "White slavery" became an issue following W. T. Stead's controversial exposure of the sale of girls to brothel owners in Europe in the *Pall Mall Gazette* in 1885. The Criminal Law Amendment Act of the same year legislated against the procuring of young girls to work as prostitutes. Stead's reports were published as *The Maiden Tribute of Modern Babylon*.

25. Réglementation was similarly opposed by post-abolitionist social purity movements in America. See Pivar, *Purity Crusade*; Pivar, *Purity and Hygiene*; Hobson, *Uneasy Virtue*.

26. On Butler, see Jordan, *Josephine Butler and the Prostitution Campaigns*; Petrie, *A Singular Iniquity*.

27. See Logan, *Fallenness*, 14, 127.

women leave prostitution, but distinguished between those who were willing to change and those who were not, the latter being thought to be beyond help. On the other hand, Butler and her followers were suspicious of attempts to make people moral by force and were alarmed at the harsh views of the purity campaigners.[28]

Despite increasing awareness that the "problem of prostitution" is more complex than previously thought, Christian responses have continued mainly to focus on the sex workers themselves rather than the male users or even the pimps and traffickers. It can come as some surprise to learn that the last of the Dublin Magdalen laundries, which effectively subjected "morally suspect" women to slave labor, was closed in the middle of the twentieth century. The stigma and fear surrounding women in prostitution persists. Women continue to be categorized as "good" and "bad," "pure" and "impure," and those who are involved in prostitution are viewed by many as "bad," or at best "damaged." Margaret Guider, for example, who worked amongst the poor in Brazil, reports women in prostitution being denied the Eucharist on the grounds that they are sinners, and denied pastoral care by priests unwilling to compromise their reputations by associating with them.[29] Some Christians fear that if they come to services they will "destroy of the image of the church."[30] Often, suspicions are voiced that women who become victims of sex trafficking are somehow to blame for their circumstances. In most churches, however, the subject of prostitution is seldom if ever discussed. It is considered distasteful—hardly the subject of polite conversation. The ideas so skillfully captured by Maupassant have dominated Christian thinking for centuries, are still present in many circles, and need to be re-examined.

4. IS PROSTITUTION MORALLY WRONG?

For the most part, the traditional view of the church has been that prostitution is morally wrong. However, this has been challenged by ethicists, and in fact the question is far more complicated than we might expect. In order to explore it, we will consider four propositions that are commonly used to argue that prostitution is morally wrong—the traditional belief that sexuality should have its expression only in marriage, the link

28. Bland, *Banishing the Beast*, xiii–xx, 95–122.

29. Guider, *Daughters of Rahab*.

30. Brock and Thistlethwaite, *Casting Stones*, 235.

between prostitution and disease, the view that prostitution is harmful to those involved, and the question of the relationship between the body and personhood. We will examine each one in turn.[31]

Proposition 1: Sexuality Should Have Its Expression Only within Marriage

The first argument often made against prostitution is that sexuality should have its expression only within marriage. However, there are several problems with this position. Firstly, there is a difficulty with the definition of marriage. For most Christians, marriage means a lifelong, monogamous, faithful contract between equals, entered into voluntarily. However, this is not the only view, for understandings vary from culture to culture. In some, polygamy is acceptable, in others arranged marriages are the norm. So too, the purpose of marriage varies—while we may like to think that marriage is exclusively for people who love each other, in many cultures, the need for social and financial security is a much more important motivation for entering into a marriage contract. "Love" is a secondary consideration, and may even be deemed a hindrance to good social order.[32]

Even if we work on the premise of a Western form of marriage, which is entered into voluntarily, it may not necessarily be the case that marriage is always a "good thing." Many marriages become very unhappy indeed, and married women can find themselves abused and practically enslaved, whether they entered into the arrangement voluntarily or not. Because of this, the morality of marriage has often come under scrutiny. A common argument for monogamous marriage is that it protects women from becoming the objects of male lust. However, in 1869 J. S. Mill suggested that for women marriage is akin to slavery—by its very nature, it cannot be an equal relationship.[33] Simone de Beauvoir argued that a married woman

31. Here I am largely dependent on Richards, "Commercial Sex and the Rights of the Person." See also Ericsson, "Charges against Prostitution"; Primoratz, *Ethics and Sex,* 88–109.

32. See Coontz, *Marriage, A History.*

33. Mill, *The Subjection of Women,* 32–33. Kant had taken the view that monogamy gives women freedom from a degrading existence as the objects of male lust. See *Anthropology from a Pragmatic Point of View,* 210–11.

merely becomes the "vassal" of her husband, losing any independence to which she might once have aspired.[34]

It must be admitted that the ideas of marriage and finance are very closely related. In many societies, women marry to escape poverty, or at least in order to ensure survival. While in the West the choice to marry may not be as obviously related to money, it is true that marriage does affect one's financial situation. The close relationship between marriage and economics led Friedrich Engels to argue that as long as private property existed, there could be no such thing as marriage entered into on the basis of romantic love. Indeed, given the unequal place of women in society, Engels suggested that there is little difference between marriage and prostitution. For Engels, the marriage of convenience,

> turns often enough into the crassest prostitution—sometimes of both partners, but far more commonly of the woman who only differs from the ordinary courtesan in that she does not let out her body on piecework as a wage worker, but sells it once for all into slavery.[35]

Bertrand Russell took a similar view: "Marriage is for woman the commonest mode of livelihood, and the total amount of undesired sex endured by women is probably greater in marriage than in prostitution."[36]

Even if we do not take such a cynical view of sexual relations within marriage as Russell, and see the married state as a relationship between two people of equal status, it has to be acknowledged that ideas are changing. Many choose to cohabit rather than marry, and divorce is much more common than it used to be. Increasingly, the traditional idea that marriage is between a male and female is questioned, as the introduction of homosexual marriage in many countries attests.

If we cannot assume that everyone is agreed as to the good of marriage, or even what marriage is, we also cannot presuppose universal assent

34. De Beauvoir, *The Second Sex*, 445–501.

35. Engels, *The Origin of the Family, Private Property and the State*, 102. Karl Marx thought that prostitution is "only a specific expression of the general prostitution of the labourer," and an example of the capitalist commercialization of all personal relationships. Prostitution, on this view, would end when inequality and poverty came to an end (*Economic and Philosophic Manuscripts of 1844*, 33). Writing anonymously in 1892, the sociologist Georg Simmel argued that prostitution would disappear when free love, rather than monogamous marriage, became the norm for sexual expression. See Frisby and Featherstone, *Simmel on Culture*, 262–70.

36. Russell, *Marriage and Morals*, 101–2.

to the view that the expression of sexuality should take place only within its confines. Many have argued that the traditional view of monogamous, sexually faithful marriage is an unrealistic ideal that cannot be upheld, and that it is unfair to those for whom marriage is somehow not available— whether due, say, to some form of disability or widowhood.

Traditionally, too, the church has maintained that sex should be associated with procreation, only to be engaged in by married couples when there is the intention of conceiving children. But this must also mean that married couples who engage in sexual activity knowing that they cannot have children are behaving immorally, and this seems absurd. Moreover, for many, the rearing of children need no longer be associated with marriage: artificial insemination makes it possible for people now to have children without being in a stable relationship or any relationship at all.

Proposition 2: Prostitution Violates the Integrity of the Person

The second argument we must consider is that the person who engages in prostitution reduces his or her body to a thing, to a commodity. If one treats one's person as a thing, this means that one fails to respect one's self. This Kantian view finds the idea of prostitution morally problematic because it considers that the body is a means rather than an end in itself. The body and the person cannot be seen separately, and to surrender oneself to another is to treat one's body as a thing. It is, therefore, *prima facie* wrong to sell the body—any part of it—even a tooth. To sell one's tooth is to sell part of one's person. Thus, when the prostitute works, her body is alienated to the will of another, and the integrity of her moral personality is undermined. Moreover, according to Kant,

> To let one's person out on hire and to surrender it to another for the satisfaction of his sexual desire in return for money is the depth of infamy. The underlying moral principle is that man is not his own property and cannot do with his body what he will. The body is part of the self; in its togetherness with the self it constitutes the person; a man cannot make of his person a thing, and this is exactly what happens in *vaga libido*. This manner of satisfying sexual desire is, therefore, not permitted by the rules of morality.[37]

37. Kant, *Lectures on Ethics*, 165–66.

Kant's view helps to voice the intuition of many that prostitution, even if regulated in the way that many suggest, is morally wrong. However, the idea of the essential unity of mind and body can lead to problems if taken to extremes. As Richards points out, most people would not say that giving blood (and other body parts, within limits) undermines one's personhood. One can hardly say that the blood donor becomes the slave of the recipient who now "owns" part of his body.

Fabre approaches Kant's view from another perspective. She objects that women who work as prostitutes cannot be said to be selling themselves, because the self cannot be "reduced to corporeality":

> It is true of course, that we construct our identity, our sense of ourselves, as sexual beings; but just as there is more to ourselves than our body, there is much more to our Identity than our sexual construction, such as our moral beliefs, our relationship with our family, our long-term plans and attachments, and so on.[38]

In other words, Kant's view implies that people who work in prostitution are somehow less than human, which is clearly not the case. In fact, it could be said that it would be an act of moral worth for a woman to prostitute herself if she believes it is for the greater good. Such is surely the case with Butterball—who sleeps with the German officer not for money in the first instance (although we are not told whether she is paid for her services or not), but still with a specific aim—the release of her companions. Moreover, his hyper-individualistic view of the integrity of the body and person would not cut any ice in Eastern societies in which the identity of the person is not constituted by notions of the self but in terms of the family, village, or tribal unit. There are today many women who view it as their moral responsibility to prostitute themselves, however distasteful they may find it, for the sake of their impoverished families.

Proposition 3: Prostitution is Responsible for the Spread of Sexually Transmitted Diseases

Prostitution has often been frowned upon because it is considered to be responsible in large part for the spread of venereal diseases and HIV/AIDS. As we have seen, this notion formed the rationale for the Contagious Diseases Acts of the 1860s. Prostitutes were blamed for the high instance of

38. Fabre, *Whose Body Is It Anyway*, 173.

venereal disease amongst the military, and the Acts gave authorities the right to subject them to compulsory examination, detention, and treatment. "Lock" hospitals were set up for the purpose of incarcerating these "fallen women" whose moral failure was considered to have brought about their diseased condition and the risk to the armed forces.[39] The clients of prostitutes were considered to be at risk from their contact with the women—but it was not thought to be necessary or even prudent to examine the soldiers themselves, or to try to curtail their activities.

However, as Butler and her colleagues argued, disease is also spread by the clients. We cannot blame one group to the exclusion of the other. Nor is it true to say that if prostitution were to stop, there would be no more sexually transmitted diseases. Promiscuity of any sort can lead to venereal infection. As we shall see, many contend that legalization might alleviate some of the problems associated with prostitution. With regard to sexually transmitted diseases, it is argued that if prostitution were to become a recognized profession, and regular health checks made compulsory for both prostitutes and clients, early detection and treatment would curb the incidence of venereal disease, at least within this section of society. However, it is by no means certain that all prostitutes and clients would submit themselves to such regulation. Many vulnerable people stumble into clandestine prostitution as a result of extreme need and are less likely to register for health checks. Moreover, with regard to AIDS, as Pisani argues, it is not so much prostitution that is responsible for the spread of the disease but certain practices, including drug injection, that render individuals more susceptible to the virus.[40]

Proposition 4: Prostitution Is Harmful

The fourth line of argument—that prostitution is harmful—is closely related to the third. Prostitution is associated with criminality and drugs, child abuse, and offensive attitudes towards women, making, as a British Government Home Office report has said, "victims of many of those involved in it, and of those communities in which it takes place."[41] People who live

---

39. See Walkowitz, *Prostitution and Victorian Society*, 214–32; Luddy, *Prostitution and Irish Society*, 124–55.

40. Pisani, *The Wisdom of Whores*. Pisani argues against the influential belief of the World Bank that AIDS is caused by poverty.

41. See the UK Home Office report *Paying the Price*. The report goes on to list,

in prostitution areas often complain about disorderly conduct, harassment of women who are not working in prostitution, and loss of business for merchants.[42] With regard to the workers themselves, there is a good deal of evidence to suggest that prostitution is an unpleasant and dangerous occupation. The high incidence of rapes, beatings, and psychological abuse from clients and pimps has led Melissa Farley, who has conducted extensive research into the health of women involved in prostitution, to conclude that they may not only suffer much physical harm, but also post-traumatic stress disorder and depression.[43] David Richards' view that prostitution is neither unpleasant nor harmful, but may actually be sexually fulfilling for women, is a minority one.[44]

Here again, the case is often made that legalization would solve these problems. Jeremy Sandford, for example, argues for the licensing and regulation of prostitution on the basis that it has the potential to be dangerous in the same way that driving a car or flying an aeroplane might be.[45] Prostitution would be considered as a job, no different from any other, with workplace regulations, taxation, and pensions. Police protection would be put in place, finances monitored, the role of pimp rendered obsolete, and workers able to choose their clients. With the controls outlined, the prostitute would not be harmed (or at least would be at much less risk), and would gain respect as a professional woman.[46]

Indeed, some argue that prostitution could be a reasonable choice for women who are otherwise unskilled and find it difficult to find employment. In an increasingly technology-based society, legalized prostitution would provide work for many and lift them out of poverty.[47] In this line of argument, the ability to provide sexual release to others is considered an asset that can be sold; so long as the risks and hazards are taken into account,

---

among other things, the nuisance caused by noise, litter, and harassment, and states that prostitution undermines "neighbourhood renewal," and has links with drug abuse and criminality, the spread of infection, the abuse of children, and harmful attitudes to women.

42. Weitzer, "The Politics of Prostitution in America."

43. See the collection of essays in Farley, *Prostitution, Trafficking and Traumatic Stress*; Coy, *Prostitution, Harm and Gender*. Also, De Marneffe, *Liberalism and Prostitution*.

44. Richards, "Commercial Sex," 1266.

45. Sandford, *Prostitutes: Portraits of People*, 164.

46. Bindman, *Redefining Prostitution as Sex Work*.

47. Califa, "Whoring in Utopia."

it may make sense to earn a living from it, in the same way that one does from having a musical or artistic talent.[48]

A related view is that there may be a "positive good" in prostitution—that it provides a service to the community. For example, it is argued that prostitutes can enable people who do not or cannot find sexual partners (for whatever reason, perhaps through disability or illness of some sort) to find sexual release and solace.[49] Another strand of this argument is that prostitutes make an important contribution to the stability of marriage and society—men who do not want to have affairs but for some reason are dissatisfied with sex within their marriage are more likely to stay with their wives if they visit prostitutes. It is also suggested that prostitution reduces sexual crimes—the availability of prostitutes may mean that those sexually frustrated men are less likely to commit rape.[50]

5. RECENT CHANGES IN OPINION

At present, then, there is little agreement on the rights and wrongs of voluntary prostitution. The traditional idea that sexual relations should be confined to marriage is increasingly under fire, while Kant's view that to prostitute oneself is "the depth of infamy" may not necessarily be true. Moreover, in the eyes of many, any dangers associated with prostitution—for workers and clients, and the public at large—could be solved by legalization and the provision of health checks and employment legislation.

The ideas outlined above are mainly concerned with the question—is it right or wrong for a woman to prostitute herself? This question has been at the basis of much Christian discussion of prostitution over the centuries. With few exceptions, the answer has been a resounding "no"—those who work in prostitution are sinners because of their promiscuous behavior. We have seen, however, that this is too simplistic a way to look at the issue. There is a case for saying that it is not always unequivocally morally wrong for women (or men, for that matter—I have been referring only to women for ease of discussion) to work in prostitution. For example, some who find

---

48. Primoratz, *Ethics and Sex*, 94

49. Richards, "Commercial Sex," 1258.

50. Current research suggests that the reasons why men visit prostitutes can range from sexual experimentation without responsibility to the need simply for someone to listen and spend time with them. See Monto, "Why Men Seek Out Prostitutes"; Sanders, *Paying for Pleasure*.

themselves in dire poverty may feel that to do so is the only way that they can support their families. In fact, to do so may be in the best interests of herself and her family—as many thousands of women who find themselves unable to make a living any other way, or find that other ways of employment pay only pitiful wages, discover.

However, the arguments outlined above point to another problem in much discussion of prostitution—the tendency to speak of those involved in prostitution in abstract and generalized terms, and to accept stereotypes as the norm.[51] Those involved in prostitution belong to a world that is "out there," divorced from the reality with which most people (let alone Christians) are familiar, promoting a "them and us" mentality. The church is respectable, while those outside are not. They also focus on the behavior of the (mainly) women themselves, ignoring the fact that prostitution would not exist were it not for those who wish to buy their services. Moreover, those involved in prostitution are, unlike the fictional Butterball, real people, with complex lives and needs.

These weaknesses of the traditional moral debate regarding prostitution have been exposed and, to some extent, addressed by recent research into the nature of sex work. Aware that those directly involved in the sex trade have seldom been heard, researchers have conducted empirical studies in which sex workers are invited to tell their own stories and experience.[52] These studies, which have mainly been carried out by feminist scholars motivated by a desire to enable marginalized women to be heard and expose systems of exploitation and abuse, have done much to challenge the stereotypes and traditional ideas. Broadly speaking, they have asked three questions: Why do people go into prostitution? What is their experience of prostitution? Should prostitution be legalized as a career option?

With regard to the first question, old ideas that women go into prostitution in order to have sex have been shown to be false.[53] Indeed, we cannot say that it is only women who become prostitutes—many men and transgender people work in the sex trade. For some, it is an active choice—this

51. As many novels and films attest, prostitutes make rather fascinating characters from Dumas' *Dame aux Camélias* to Julia Roberts' role in the movie *Pretty Woman*. Today, too, books such as Belle de Jour's *The Intimate Adventures of a London Call-Girl*, and Miss S., *Confessions of a Working Girl* sell in large numbers all over the world.

52. For example, Delacoste and Alexander, *Sex Work*; Chapkis, *Live Sex Acts*; Bernstein, *Temporarily Yours*; Brennan *What's Love Got to Do with It?*.

53. Attempts to find psychological causes (see for example Choisy, *Psychoanalysis of the Prostitute*) have largely been discredited. See Sterk, *Tricking and Tripping*, 20–24.

is the best way they can earn money to support their families, and it gives them freedom and flexibility to work when they want. Some go into prostitution because discrimination (for example, race, caste, or gender), addiction, or mental illness, mean that they cannot find other means of employment. In India, the caste system means that prostitution is the only option for some women. Poor education and extreme poverty can also mean that women have few opportunities for other forms of work. As Brock and Thistlethwaite note,

> The particular configurations of developing industrialized societies in Asia create a market environment that virtually forces many young women to choose sex industry work. The central issues here are governmental economic policies, social disruption, corporate practices, international development policies, militarization, and family structure, as well as male domination and oppression.[54]

For many caught up in this situation, the criminalization of prostitution means that they cannot look to the police for help if they find themselves in danger, and if they do, they may themselves be arrested or abused. The stigma and shame which are often attached to what they do add to their burden.

Experiences of prostitution are also varied. Some report that it is a good way to earn a living and feel that they are offering a valuable service to their customers. These reports tend to come from women who work in legalized brothels or for themselves. Street workers, on the other hand, tend to speak of poor working conditions in which they fear physical attack and rape. Many studies show that those involved in prostitution have different perceptions of their work, depending not only on their personal circumstances, but on their culture and setting. Prostitution in East Asia is quite different from that found in America or Australia, for example.[55]

These empirical studies have also been a major part of a debate among feminists as to whether prostitution is exploitative towards women or not. In other words, should prostitution be seen as an opportunity for women to take control of their own bodies and lives, or as an opportunity for men to treat them as objects and slaves?[56] Some argue that voluntary prostitution

54. Brock and Thistlelthwaite, *Casting Stones*, 14.

55. See, for example, Sahni et al., *Prostitution and Beyond*; Saeed, *Taboo!*; Kempadoo and Doezema, *Global Sex Workers*; Maher et al., *Sex Work*; Gangoli, "Prostitution in India"; Truong, *Sex, Money and Morality*, 131–57.

56. Simmons, "Theorising Prostitution," 146.

should be considered a career choice like any other. In this line of thinking, women who choose to become prostitutes are seen as in control of their sexuality, exercising their freedom and taking power for themselves. The argument is that they are providing a service for which there is a demand, and that in doing so they are asserting their autonomy as women. Any danger that may be involved will be helped by legalization.[57]

On the other hand, there are those who believe that prostitution is a form of abuse, another aspect of male domination over women.[58] This more common view has a long pedigree. Simone de Beauvoir believed that the prostitute is a scapegoat, who, as long as she is denied the rights of a person, "sums up all the forms of feminine slavery at once."[59] Today, Evelina Giobbe argues in similar vein. Prostitution, she writes, "is nothing less than the commercialization of the sexual abuse and inequality that women suffer in the traditional family and can be nothing more."[60]

For Kathleen Barry, prostitution is an extreme form of sexual slavery that reduces women to expendable bodies; she believes this will increase in a society that is becoming ever more sexualized.[61] A more extreme view is expressed by Dworkin, who argues that the man who seeks out a prostitute is exercising his hatred of women in general, abusing them, and taking pleasure in the fact of their weakness and his own power.[62] On this view, it is impossible to speak of prostitution in terms of choice:

> Until women, globally, are less marginalized, no one can realistically view prostitution as a "choice"—even if it may sometimes be an immediate tool for survival. This, in fact, is the inherent paradox of prostitution: that a social practice involving known violence, including possible rape, beatings, and even death, can ever be seen as a rational solution.[63]

The view that prostitution constitutes abuse has been endorsed by women who have been involved in prostitution. The pressure group WHISPER (Women Hurt In Systems of Prostitution Engaged in Revolt) speaks

57. See, for example, Delacoste and Alexander, *Sex Work*; Chapkis, *Live Sex Acts*.

58. E.g., Dworkin, "Prostitution and Male Supremacy"; MacKinnon, *Feminism Unmodified*.

59. De Beauvoir, *The Second Sex*, 569.

60. Giobbe, "Confronting the Liberal Lies about Prostitution," 80.

61. Barry, *The Prostitution of Sexuality*.

62. Dworkin, "*Prostitution and Male Supremacy*," 139–51.

63. Johnson, "Ain't I a Human?" 38.

for women who have been harmed by their experiences. In the words of Sarah Wynter,

> We, the women of WHISPER, reject the lie that women freely choose prostitution from a whole array of economic alternatives that exist under civil equality. . . . We reject the lie that turning tricks is sexual pleasure or agency for women. We reject the lie that women can and do become wealthy in systems of prostitution. We reject the lie that women control and are empowered in systems of prostitution.[64]

However, this view is not universal amongst sex workers.[65] Gail Pheterson, an advocate for the rights of prostitutes, argues for the decriminalization of voluntary prostitution, and resents the idea that women should be "rescued," even by feminists. She complains that "[i]nstitutional exploitation of prostitutes on the one side and ideological salvation of prostitutes on the other squeeze whores between two lethally legitimate mechanisms of control."[66]

Feminists who argue against prostitution as a legitimate choice for women are, in Phetersen's view, no better than the nineteenth-century social purists who wanted to help women to change their ways. They are depriving women of autonomy and ultimately colluding with a society that wants to dominate women. On these grounds too, some feminists speak of the "myth" of sex trafficking, seeing it as a construct promoting ideas of women as subordinate to and victims of men.[67]

Both feminists and those involved in prostitution, then, are divided in their opinions as to whether it is good for women. Some think that women can prostitute themselves without harm, arguing that it can be empowering for women both financially and sexually. Others, however, take the view that prostitution is nothing more than commercialized misogyny, an unacceptable exploitation of women.

The current lack of agreement as to the nature of prostitution is reflected in various approaches to legislation, and while the most common

64. Delacoste and Alexander, *Sex Work*, 269.

65. Peterson-Iyer summarizes the two approaches to prostitution amongst organized prostitutes as "liberal/contractarian" versus "domination/subjection"; see "Prostitution: A Feminist Ethical Analysis." She takes the latter approach.

66. Pheterson, *A Vindication of the Rights of Whores*, 15. See also Lerum, "Twelve-Step Feminism Makes Sex Workers Sick."

67. See for example, Agustín, *Sex at the Margins*; Doezema, *Sex Slaves and Discourse Matters*.

response is to outlaw the sex trade, many argue for prostitution to be considered a job like any other with health checks and protection for employees who work in licensed brothels or toleration zones.[68] This approach has been pioneered in Holland and in some counties of Nevada. Legalization is distinct from decriminalization, which has been adopted in New Zealand. This means that brothels remain unlicensed, but sex workers employed in them are subject to the employment legislation applicable in any other area of work. Both approaches are designed to protect prostitutes, not only from harm from clients and exploitation by pimps and madams, but also from having a police record that will make finding other work difficult. At the same time, influenced by feminist arguments that prostitution is exploitation of women (and that such exploitation should not be legalized), some governments are exploring the idea of prosecuting clients rather than the women themselves.[69] This approach has been adopted in Scandinavia with some success, and several other countries have either followed suit or are considering doing so. It remains to be seen what the long-term consequences will be.[70] However, this approach does address the problem of blaming women for the existence of prostitution, and shifts responsibility on to the male customers.

6. CONCLUSION

I have been suggesting that it is important that Christians recognize that attitudes towards prostitution complicate the way churches respond to sex trafficking. Prejudice and simplistic preconceived ideas about prostitution as sin have blinded us to the complexity of the problem, added to the burden felt by those who are the victims of sex trafficking, and hindered balanced contribution to debates as to how to tackle it. As Maupassant's story so skillfully illustrates, reactions to prostitution tend to be characterized by ambivalence and double standards. While it is most often seen as a social problem, there are times when we are prepared to turn a blind eye to it and even see it as a necessity. Moreover, while prostitutes are stigmatized,

---

68. On current legislation see Westmarland and Gongoli, *International Approaches to Prostitution*, 1–17. See further the discussion in Williams, "Beyond Wolfenden?"

69. See for example, Brooks-Gordon and Gelsthorpe, "Hiring Bodies."

70. Skilbrei and Holmström, *Prostitution Policy in the Nordic Region*; Svanstrom, "Prostitution in Sweden."

and considered to be beyond the social pale, the behavior of the men who purchase their services is largely ignored.

A brief survey of the history of prostitution has shown that this ambivalent response to the "problem of prostitution" has been typical, not only of the Christian church but of individuals and secular states. In practice, the Christian attitude to prostitutes has tended to be twofold: either they have been shunned altogether or seen as "fallen women" who have to be protected from the vice that threatened their salvation.

We have also seen that philosophical arguments commonly made against prostitution are less than robust, and that it is possible to argue that prostitution is as legitimate an occupation as any other. For many feminist scholars, the question has moved on to be one of whether or not prostitution is fundamentally exploitative, and opinion is divided on this. This raises questions for the church as to whether prostitution should be considered sinful, and indeed whether this is the right question to be asking at all. These are important issues that must be addressed in any attempt to respond to sex trafficking.

As we turn to the biblical texts, then, we have some questions to ask of them. Is the traditional consensus that prostitution is sinful an appropriate response? We have seen that there is a "redemptive impulse" throughout Scripture with regard to slavery in general, but can we say the same for those caught up in prostitution—or does the church's tendency to stigmatize them have biblical grounding? What, if anything, can the biblical texts say to us about the current questions of whether the sex trade is exploitative or not? What, if anything, can they have to say about tackling sex trafficking?

CHAPTER 5

The Bible and Prostitution

1. INTRODUCTION

In this chapter, we will conduct a survey of biblical passages that refer to prostitution. Drawing once again on the insights gained from the abolitionists' approach to Scripture, we come to the texts from a standpoint that understands the message of Scripture to be one of God's love for his people and hatred of injustice. However, we also must acknowledge that the church has been complicit in the marginalizing and demonizing of those caught up in prostitution. So we must ask, how should the church respond to the problem of prostitution, with all its historical associations of sin, shame, and moral opprobrium? Can the Bible help us with the questions that are currently so important with regard to tackling contemporary sex trafficking?

2. PROSTITUTION IN THE OLD TESTAMENT

The *Qĕdēšîm*

Two Hebrew terms are commonly translated as "prostitute." *Zônā* refers to a woman who offers sexual services for financial reward. *Qĕdēšâ* (fem) or *qādēš* (masc) is often translated "cultic prostitute." While the meaning of *zônā* seems clear, that of *qĕdēšâ* is less obvious. The term means "holy" or "consecrated one," that is, someone who is dedicated as a servant to the cult. In ANE religions such people probably performed various services, but what these services were is rather unclear.

The Israelites may have believed that there was a sexual component to the activities of the *qĕdēšîm*. For example, in Genesis 38, Hirah thinks that Tamar is a *qĕdēšâ* attached to the cult, while Judah takes her to be a prostitute (*zônā*). Whatever the exact nature of their role, the *qĕdēšîm* are always condemned as undesirable elements bringing pagan practices into the land (1 Kgs 14:23–24; 15:11–12) and into the temple itself (2 Kgs 23:7, cf. Isa 23:18). In contemporary scholarship, the view that they were sacred prostitutes is now regarded as untenable because no evidence has been found to substantiate it, and for this reason we will focus on passages in which the term *zônā* is used.[1]

The Law

A few laws deal with prostitution directly. In Leviticus 19:29, it is stipulated that men should not make their daughters work as prostitutes, for this would profane them, depriving them of the ability to be holy. More than this, however, this lucrative practice could spread, making society "full of depravity."[2] In Leviticus 21:7, 14, priests are prohibited from marrying prostitutes, women who have been "defiled," divorcees, or widows—in other words, women who are not virgins.[3] Priests, who form the interface between the sanctuary and the people, must be meticulous as to purity. Besides adhering to ritual cleanliness instructions and food laws, they must ensure that their sexual partners are pure. They are required to marry only virgins from their own kin in order to ensure that any children are their own.[4] Further, since priests handle food that is offered to God, the behavior of their families, who also eat this food (Lev 10:14), is crucial in maintaining purity. Thus, in Leviticus 21:9 it is a capital offence for a priest's daughter to become a prostitute. Her behavior affects her father's purity (and thus that

---

1. Budin, *The Myth of Sacred Prostitution in Antiquity*; Bird, "The End of the Male Cult Prostitute."

2. Milgrom, *Leviticus 17–22*, 1699.

3. On the difficulties translating Lev 21:7 see Hartley, *Leviticus 1–27*, 343.

4. Hartley, *Leviticus*, 349.

of the sanctuary) as well as his honor. It may be that the penalty of burning is to be rid of the impurity that her prostitution brings into the cult.[5]

The prohibition against bringing the fees of a harlot, or the "price of a dog," into the sanctuary (Deut 23:18) is strange. Brueggemann suggests that business integrity is in mind here, the money earned from prostitution coming from transactions "in which the strong will always defeat the weak."[6] However, it is also possible that the proceeds from prostitution were considered unclean in the same way that money from the sale of dogs is unclean, because dogs, being scavengers, consume blood (cf. 1 Kgs 22:38).[7]

But why is the prostitute associated with uncleanness in this way? Firstly, *all* sexual activity is associated with ritual impurity—bodily fluids must be washed away prior to participation in the cult. Married couples who have sexual intercourse are considered ritually unclean until evening (Lev 15:18), as is any man who has an emission of semen. An abnormal genital discharge is very serious, requiring careful measures to ensure that others are not contaminated (Lev 15).

Anthropologically, the explanation for these laws may be that bodily fluids, such as semen or blood, when outside the body, are "matter out of place," waste material that is a source of ritual pollution.[8] Or, it may be that the close proximity of reproductive organs to the urethra renders semen unclean.[9] Secondly, women become unclean during menstruation (Lev 15:19–24), and after childbirth. In fact, women are associated with impurity from the time of their birth—giving birth to a female child renders a woman unclean for eighty days as opposed to forty days for a male child (Lev 12:1–8). As a promiscuous woman, the prostitute is ritually unclean much of the time.

Social custom would also indirectly control prostitution. There should, in theory, be no need for men to make use of prostitutes. Female slaves were assumed to be the sexual property of their masters, and it was acceptable to acquire women in battle and force them into bearing children

---

5. Burnside, *The Signs of Sin*, 125.

6. Brueggemann, *Deuteronomy*, 233. Cf. Van Der Toorn, "Female Prostitution in Payment of Vows," suggests that some women may have prostituted themselves to pay vows made to the cult (e.g., Mic 1:7).

7. Houston, *Purity and Monotheism*, 189–90; Goodfriend, "Could *keleb* in Deuteronomy 23:19 Actually Refer to a Canine?."

8. Douglas, *Purity and Danger*, but cf. Frymer-Kensky, "Pollution, Purification and Purgation in Biblical Israel."

9. See Whitekettle, "Leviticus 15:18 Reconsidered."

(Deut 21:10–14).[10] While the lawmakers did not view women as equal to men, they did have a strong sense of their inherent dignity. At least in the case of debt-bondage, there was an understanding that the sexual use of female slaves should entail a change in their status from slave to permanent member of the family (Exod 21:7–11).[11] Women who were not enslaved were under the authority and protection of their fathers until marriage, and should have no need to resort to prostitution.[12] It was thus a male responsibility to ensure that the honor of the household was maintained. Sometimes, however, a woman could find herself outside male authority, perhaps through widowhood, or divorce, or loss of parents, and in such circumstances, prostitution might be the only option.

Narratives

The existence of prostitution in Israelite society is reflected in several narratives. For example, in 1 Kings 3:16–28, two prostitutes come to Solomon to resolve a dispute in which one woman accuses the other, whose own child has died, of having stolen her baby. Solomon suggests that they cut the living child in two, thereby ensuring that the real mother identifies herself. Solomon's great wisdom is demonstrated, and the fact that the two women are prostitutes does not have any bearing on the story at all, except perhaps to show that low-status women have access to the king.[13] Similarly, Jephthah's mother is said to have been a prostitute (Judg 11:1), perhaps to emphasize the lowly origins of an influential man.[14] The reports of Samson's visit to a prostitute (Judg 16:1), his disastrous marriage, and his affair with Delilah, may be intended to show his weakness in the face of sexual temptation.[15]

---

10. See Mbuwayesango, "Canaanite Women and Israelite Women in Deuteronomy." Cf. Pressler, *The View of Women*; Anderson, *Women, Ideology and Violence*.

11. Jackson, "Biblical Laws of Slavery"; see further Kriger, *Sex Rewarded, Sex Punished*.

12. Women were not necessarily considered to be weak or morally inferior, however. They could wield considerable power in circumscribed roles as mothers and wives. See Frymer-Kensky, *In the Wake of the Goddesses*, 141–42; Meyers, *Rediscovering Eve*; Wegner, *Chattel or Person*, 37.

13. Brenner, *The Israelite Woman*, 78–83.

14. Cf. Bal, *Death and Dissymmetry*, 177–78.

15. Smith, "Samson and Delilah."

In the stories of Tamar and Rahab, however, the principal characters' association with prostitution is highly significant. In Genesis 38, Tamar, Judah's daughter-in-law, is left a childless widow. According to the law of Levirate marriage, she should be given to her deceased husband's brothers in order to ensure lineage.[16] However, the first brother refuses to comply, and dies. Judah declines to pair her off with his third son, Shelah, afraid of losing him too. When her father-in-law goes to Timnah for sheep-shearing, Tamar sits at the roadside pretending to be a prostitute, her face hidden by a veil. Judah propositions her, but since he cannot pay her, agrees to give her his seal, cord, and staff as a pledge. When Judah's friend Hirah goes to give her a goat as payment, however, Tamar is nowhere to be found. Judah decides not to pursue the matter, for fear of becoming a laughingstock. Tamar conceives, and when her pregnancy becomes known, she is accused of having "played the whore" (Gen 38:24). Judah pronounces that she must be burned to death. However, Tamar sends the seal, staff, and cord to Judah. Their owner is responsible for her pregnancy, does he recognize them? Judah does, and declares that Tamar is more righteous than he is because he did not give her to Shelah. She becomes the mother of twins, and the continuation of Judah's family is ensured.[17]

Rahab is explicitly designated as a *zônā* (Josh 2). One day two Israelite men, who have been sent into Canaan as spies, come to stay in her house. Disobeying an instruction from the king of Jericho to hand them over to him, Rahab hides them in the roof. The Canaanites, she tells them, have heard of Israel's deliverance from Egypt and are afraid of them, for they know that Yahweh has guided them. Rahab asks that her family be spared; assurance is given in return for secrecy regarding their activities. Rahab helps them to escape, and the Israelites go on to defeat and occupy Canaan. Joshua ensures that she and her family are kept safe (Josh 6:15–25).

Both narratives provide glimpses of attitudes towards prostitution in ancient society. Prostitutes are outcasts, their activities considered dishonorable. Rahab lives at the city walls in Canaan, and even when she lives in Israel, she is still known as a prostitute (Josh 6:25). Tamar's activities are considered so shameful that she is almost executed. There are double standards. The fact that the spies go to a brothel is apparently unremarkable,

---

16. Deut 25:5–10. See Westbrook, *Property and Family in Biblical Law,* 69–89; Weisberg, "The Widow of our Discontent."

17. Menn, *Judah and Tamar,* 15.

and Judah can use the services of a prostitute with impunity.[18] But there are many ironies. As feminist scholars point out, both women get the better of men in a patriarchal society: Rahab dupes the king of Canaan, and facilitates the invasion and defeat of her country by the Israelites;[19] Judah the patriarch has to declare that the woman he wronged is more righteous than he is.[20] Further, both women are outsiders who become heroines of Israel's history: Rahab is a Canaanite who recognizes Yahweh as God, and Tamar (who is a widow and possibly not an Israelite) ensures the continuation of Judah's lineage. That Tamar pretends to be a prostitute and Rahab actually is one, deepens the irony. The spies, by going straight to a brothel, put themselves and the entire project at great risk, jeopardizing God's plan. Exploiting his sexual appetite, Tamar rescues Judah from his indifference and fear.[21]

"Playing the Harlot"

The verb *zānâ*, which is often translated "play the whore," appears frequently throughout the Old Testament. However, it can be difficult to discern whether it refers to prostitution, adultery, or promiscuity. For example, has Tamar been recognized on the road to Timnah, or is she being accused of adultery (Gen 38:24)? *Zānâ*, therefore, may not always refer to prostitution. Following Phyllis Bird, we will assume that "fornication or illicit extramarital relations should be the starting point for interpreting any given use."[22] This has important implications for many other texts. For example, Leviticus 21:9, which is usually understood as stipulating that a priest's daughter who becomes a prostitute (*liznôt*) should be burned to death, may refer to promiscuity or simply sex before marriage. The same caveat must be applied with regard to Deuteronomy 22:19–21, in which a woman who is found not to be a virgin when she marries is said to have "played the harlot" (*liznôt*) while still under her father's authority.[23]

18. *Pace* Hess, *Joshua*, 83, who insists that no sexual activity takes place.

19. See Kuan and Le Tran, "Reading Race Reading Rehab"; Klein, *The Triumph of Irony in the Book of Judges.*

20. See, e.g., Smith, "The Story of Tamar," 25; See also Susan Niditch, "The Wronged Woman Righted."

21. Petersen, *Reading Women's Stories*, 119–64.

22. Bird, "To Play the Harlot." See also Miller, "A Critical Response."

23. Frymer-Kensky, "Virginity in the Bible," 79–96.

Most often, the verb is used metaphorically, usually with regard to idolatrous behavior, in which fulfilling one's own desires takes precedence over obedience to Yahweh. This includes worshipping pagan gods (e.g., Exod 34:15–16; Judg 2:17; 8:33; cf. Num 25:1–3) or consulting mediums (Lev 20:6). It may be that the metaphor originated in reaction to the Canaanite cult and its preoccupation with fertility.[24] To go after the Baals is to "play the harlot." The idea is developed in the prophetic literature. In Isaiah 1:21, Jerusalem is described as a "harlot" because, though she is religiously observant, there is injustice in the city, the root cause of which is dabbling in pagan ritual (1:29, cf. Isa 57:3). Tyre's lucrative trade in luxury items has led her to "prostitute herself" (Isa 23:15–17). As Otto Kaiser notes, "commerce takes up any contact which it hopes will bring in money."[25] In Nahum 3, Nineveh is likened to a prostitute who will be humiliated for her debauched behavior.

The harlotry metaphor is often juxtaposed with the idea of the covenant relationship as a marriage between Yahweh and his people.[26] In Hosea, the prophet is instructed to marry a woman, Gomer, who is described as a "woman of promiscuity" ('ēšet zĕnûnîm).[27] Israel (Hos 4:11–14) has become ensnared by Baal worship, bringing a "spirit of fornication" (rûah zĕnûnîm) into the land. She is behaving like a prostitute who is looking for customers (2:5). Gomer, who represents Israel, is never explicitly called a zōnâ, but she must be brought to heel, and turn back to Yahweh, and so is threatened with stripping and exposure, and even death (2:3).

In Jeremiah, Israel is said to have played the whore "under every green tree"—that is, she is worshipping the Baals (2:20). She has been lustful, forgetting everything Yahweh has done for her, and harming the "innocent poor" in the process (2:34). She has lived as a prostitute with many lovers (3:1–3) and has become brazen. Yahweh divorces Israel (3:8), but wants her to admit her guilt and return to him (3:12). Harlotry of this nature pollutes the land (3:1), which must be cleansed (13:27).

This imagery is taken to extremes by Ezekiel who protests against political and religious betrayal of the covenant. Israel's harlotry is portrayed as nymphomania, for she rejects payment and so "subjugates her identity

---

24. Ortlund, *Whoredom*, 32.

25. Kaiser, *Isaiah 13–39*, 171.

26. On the marriage metaphor see Abma, *Bonds of Love*.

27. This could refer to either prostitution or unfaithfulness. For the view that Gomer is a prostitute see, for example, Hornsby, "Israel Has Become a Worthless Thing."

to her sexual drive."[28] In chapter 16, Jerusalem is depicted as an abandoned baby, rescued and nurtured by Yahweh, who enters into a covenant with her. She becomes a beautiful queen, but forgets Yahweh, and becomes a prostitute. She makes idols out of her jewelry, and even sacrifices her children. She has many lovers, including Egyptians, Assyrians, and Chaldeans. Yahweh threatens to humiliate her and punish her, warning her that her customers will rob her and leave her to the cruelty of the mob, who will stone her and cut her to pieces. She will lose her distinctive reputation amongst the nations, and be considered worse than Sodom and other cities. But when Yahweh re-establishes the covenant and makes atonement for her actions, she will remember and be ashamed.

In Ezekiel 23, two sisters, daughters of Yahweh, Ohola (Samaria) and Oholibah (Jerusalem), are described as having become prostitutes in Egypt. Oholah lusts after and gives herself to the elite young men of Assyria and worships their idols. Delivered into their hands by Yahweh, Oholah is humiliated and killed. Oholibah is even more depraved. As well as lusting after the Assyrians she invites the Babylonians to come to her, and yearns to return to Egypt. Yahweh warns Oholibah that she will suffer in the same way as Samaria: her lovers will cut off her nose and ears, strip and rob her, and seize her children. It is even suggested that she will be raped (23:29). Her anguish will be such that she will drunkenly tear her own breasts out (23:34).

Since "playing the harlot" can refer to promiscuity or any illicit sexual activity, the phrase denotes behavior that will undermine the integrity of the family and the land as a whole. It can also refer to idolatry—rebellion against Yahweh, which will lead to political disaster for Israel and, often, injustice and suffering for the poor. When used alongside the marriage metaphor, the harlot figure is sharply contrasted with Yahweh's faithful love, and his longing to restore his covenant relationship.[29]

Wisdom

The dramatic rhetoric of the prophets stands in sharp contrast to the measured tones of wisdom literature, whose counsel reflects centuries of experience and learning. In Proverbs, the aim is to teach young men not to be led astray into foolish behavior, which can only lead to ruin. Sexual

28. Halbertal and Margalit, *Idolatry*, 17.

29. See, for example, Swanepoel, "Ezekiel 16."

misconduct in general leads to individual ruin and social disorder. In chapters 1–9, there are warnings against wicked men who will lead a young man into crime, against laziness, and corrupt dealings. There are also warnings concerning the wiles of the "strange woman," whose aim is to entice him into adultery. This woman, who is married, is the opposite of Lady wisdom, who will honor and exalt him if he seeks her counsel (4:8).[30] The "strange woman," however, can ruin him. Lacking modesty, she dresses like a prostitute (Prov 7:10). If the young man were to take up with her, he would bring financial and social disaster, even death, upon himself. Indeed it would be better to buy the services of a prostitute than to become involved with a married woman (Prov 6:26)—"for a prostitute's fee is only a loaf of bread, but the wife of another stalks a man's very life." As McKane notes, "it is one thing to resort to a harlot and pay her a small fee; it is quite another to set up as a mistress another man's wife who expected style and luxury as a reward."[31]

But it is mistaken to infer from this that using prostitutes is approved of, for elsewhere, this is described as folly: what seems attractive can be dangerous and destructive. Proverbs 23:27–28 describes the harlot as "a deep pit" from which there is no escape—her client will be like a trapped animal.[32] Similarly, in Proverbs 29:3 keeping company with prostitutes is likely to result in the loss of both money and reputation.

Conclusion on Prostitution in the Old Testament

The undesirability of prostitution in society is mainly expressed in cultic terms. However, prostitution is not just a ritual sin, it is a moral sin, for it puts the whole "land" at risk of pollution.[33] Why this should be so is not clear in the texts, but we can perhaps explain it by means of the whoring metaphor. If going after the Baals introduces elements foreign to the worship of Yahweh, so too the prostitute's promiscuity threatens the biological integrity of the people. Just as seed is sown on land, so seed is "sown" in a

---

30. See, for example, Camp, *Wisdom and the Feminine*; Murphy, "Wisdom and Eros in Proverbs 1–9."

31. McKane, *Proverbs*, 330.

32. Ibid., 391.

33. For this distinction see Klawans, *Impurity and Sin in Ancient Judaism*.

woman. The promiscuous woman's body receives foreign "seed," and the land is put at risk because family lines can no longer be trusted to be pure.[34]

For men, adultery brings outright condemnation, but using prostitutes is considered merely unwise.[35] Regulation is not effected through direct prohibition, except in the case of the priesthood (cf. Hos 4:13–14), but rather through associations with impurity, the cultural demands on men to maintain the honor of their families, and the marginalizing of prostitutes themselves, who, because of their uncleanness, are feared and shunned.[36] But prostitutes are also dangerous because they do not conform to societal norms. An independent woman who operates outside the authority of a male may not be an adulteress, but she is suspect.[37] Indeed, any female sexual activity that is not directed at securing male heirs for a husband, is likely to be branded as "whoring." The popular view of the prostitute as unclean and dangerous is exploited in the prophets' use of the harlotry metaphor in which she becomes the symbol of, and scapegoat for, all that is inimical to Yahweh and his cult.[38]

However, certain subversive voices undermine this prevailing cultural view. In the narratives of Rahab and Tamar, double standards are exposed, and the idea of the prostitute as sinner *par excellence* overturned, both women becoming mothers in the Davidic dynasty. Moreover, there is a strong tradition in the legal and wisdom traditions that teaches male responsibility for maintaining the dignity and sexual integrity of women, including slaves, as well as their own behavior. The stigmatization of prostitutes is balanced, to some extent, by attempts to protect women from exploitation.

3. PROSTITUTION IN THE NEW TESTAMENT

The Greek equivalent to *zōnâ* is *pornē*. The *pornē* is usually a slave, forced to work as a prostitute.[39] In this section we will consider those passages in

---

34. Shields, *Circumscribing the Prostitute*, 61; Berquist, *Controlling Corporeality*, 67. See further Lerner, *The Creation of Patriarchy*.

35. *Pace* Countryman, *Dirt, Greed and Sex*, 166, who sees the advice in Proverbs 5:15–23 as reproof.

36. Koltun-Fromm, *Hermeneutics of Holiness*, 16.

37. Streete, *The Strange Woman*, 74; cf. Schulte, "Beobachten zum Begriff der Zônâ."

38. See Ricoeur, *Symbolism of Evil*, 25–46.

39. In classical Greece, the *pornē* was a slave, while the *hetaera* was a freewoman

which the term appears, but as we shall see, the subject is far less prominent in the New Testament than Christian tradition might lead us to expect.[40] The related term *porneia* is sometimes translated as "prostitution," but has a broader meaning of illicit sexual behavior.[41]

First-century Judaism condemned women in prostitution and the men who use them.[42] In the Greco-Roman world, however, the use of prostitutes was an accepted part of life: they worked in brothels, as street walkers, and as entertainment at temple and civic occasions. Prostitutes themselves, and their pimps, were generally considered to be dishonorable.[43]

The Gospels

Two women in the Gospels have traditionally been thought to be prostitutes—the woman who anoints Jesus, and Mary Magdalene. However, there is a lack of solid textual support. The designation of the woman who anoints Jesus in Luke 7:36–50 as a "sinner" has often been taken to suggest that she is a prostitute, as has the reference to her long loose hair. However, unbound hair need not imply prostitution, and the term "sinner" could denote any behavior deemed unacceptable by the religious authorities.[44] Her presence in the room suggests she is not a "public" woman but belongs to the household, perhaps as a slave.[45] The parallel narratives do not call her a sinner (Mark 14:3–9; Matt 26:6–13; John 12:1–8). In the Markan and Matthean accounts she is described as poor, and commended for her generous prophetic action, while in John 12:1–8, she is said to be Mary

---

who worked as a prostitute. See Cohen, "Free and Unfree Sexual Work." On *hetaera* see Davidson, *Courtesans and Fishcakes*, 109–36.

40. While the NIV translates *malakoi* (1 Cor 6:9) as male prostitute, it is more likely that the term refers to same-sex activity in general (though not "homosexuality" as such for there was no notion of sexual orientation in those days). See the discussion in Thistleton, *First Epistle to the Corinthians*, 447–51.

41. See Harper, "Porneia."

42. Lemos, *Marriage Gifts and Social Change*.

43. See McGinn, "Zoning Shame in the Roman City." On prostitution in the Roman Empire see further McGinn, *Prostitution, Sexuality and the Law*.

44. Fiorenza, *In Memory of Her*, 128; Cosgrove, "A Woman's Unbound Hair in the Greco-Roman World."

45. Hornsby, "The Woman Is a Sinner"; Corley, *Private Women, Public Meals*, 121–30, suggests she might have been a slave.

of Bethany. It appears that the tradition behind these narratives does not remember her as a prostitute.

The popular belief that Mary Magdalene was a prostitute is now discredited.[46] The (scant) data are as follows. In Luke 8:1–3, she is said to have walked closely with Jesus, supported his ministry out of her own resources, and to have had seven demons cast out. Elsewhere, she is recorded as being present at the crucifixion (Mark 15:40–41; Matt 27:55–56; John 19:25), and at Jesus' burial (Matt 27:61; Mark 15:47). In the Synoptic Gospels she goes with others to anoint Jesus' dead body (Mark 16:1–2; Luke 24:1–10; cf. Matt 28:1). According to John 20:1–18, however, she goes alone, and is the first witness to the resurrection. Some have thought that the risen Jesus' instruction to her in John 20:17, which has often been translated "do not touch me" (*mē mou haptou*), has a sexual component to it. However, the Greek is much closer to "do not hold on to me."[47] The suggestion that the "seven demons" were sexual in nature is without foundation.

The term *pornē* appears only three times in the Gospels (Matt 21:31, 32; Luke 15:30). Having told the story of the two sons (Matt 21:28–29), in which one son refuses to work in his father's vineyard but later does, while the second says he will work but does not, Jesus asks the chief priests and elders which one did the father's will. They answer that the first one did so. Jesus responds by saying that tax-collectors and prostitutes are going into the kingdom of God ahead of them: the "unrighteous" have believed John the Baptist's message while religious leaders have not. Like the brother who initially seems disobedient, prostitutes and tax collectors are hardly the first people one would think of as belonging to God's kingdom. Those who think they are righteous should take heed. The other occurrence is in the Parable of the Prodigal Son (Luke 15:30). When the son returns home, the older brother accuses him of having squandered his inheritance on prostitutes. Whether this is true or not is not disclosed; Jesus may have used a common idea for rhetorical effect.[48] Nevertheless, the prodigal's behavior is a prime example of the failure to heed the warning of Proverbs 29, and the older son is scornful. Their father, however, offers unconditional forgiveness.

46. In addition to the resources cited in chapter 4, see D'Angelo, "Reconstructing 'Real' Women from Gospel Literature."

47. See Attridge, "'Don't Be Touching Me.'"

48. See Calon, "*Adulescentes* and *Meretrices*." Spending money on prostitutes was a "stereotypical feature of prodigality common in Graeco-Roman comedy."

In both instances, prostitutes appear as illustrations of people commonly classed as sinners. Jesus is not suggesting, however, that they should be shunned. In fact, his dealings with women in general suggest the opposite. In first-century Palestine, women were considered to be inferior.[49] Jesus, however, treats them as equals, giving them senior roles in his ministry.[50] Moreover, he does not abide by purity conventions. He allows the woman with the flow of blood to touch him (Matt 9:20–22; Mark 5:25–34; Luke 8:43–48; cf. Lev 15:25–30), and praises her faith despite her contravention of purity regulations.[51] He accepts the Samaritan woman at the well as she is, without condemning her for her many husbands, and she becomes the first to tell her people about him (John 4:1–30). As the parable of the two sons illustrates, God's salvific work is inclusive—even of those abhorred by the religious authorities.[52]

Paul

The Hebrew Scriptures do not prohibit the use of prostitutes. Paul, however, is clear:

> Do you not know that your bodies are members of Christ? Should
> I therefore take the members of Christ and make them members
> of a prostitute? Never! (1 Cor 6:15)

But why does he object so strongly? It seems that some in the Corinthian congregation thought that they could behave as they pleased (1 Cor 6:12). Indulging the appetites was natural—"Food is meant for the stomach and the stomach for food" (6:13). Since the body would one day be destroyed, it was unimportant what one did with it. Paul protests; the body is not meant for immorality, but for serving the Lord. Following one's appetites blindly is inconsistent with being a believer, for several reasons. Firstly, their bodies will not be destroyed, but will be raised up at the end times, just as the Lord's body was raised at the resurrection (6:14). Secondly, since believers' bodies are not "just" their bodies—they are "members of Christ" (6:15)—they cannot consider themselves to be physically separate from him. Thirdly, there is no split between their bodies and their spirits. They

---

49. See Ilan, *Jewish Women in Greco-Roman Palestine*.

50. See for example, Beirne, *Women and Men in the Fourth Gospel*.

51. Miller, *Women in Mark's Gospel*, 60.

52. Thompson, "Gathered at the Table."

are spiritually and physically united with Christ (6:17). Thus, sex is much more than a mere physical experience. Citing Genesis 2:24, Paul states that an encounter with a prostitute means that the two people become "one flesh." And since flesh is not separate from spirit, any sexual relationship must entail spiritual union. Thus, the man who engages in transient, commercial sexual encounters sins "against his own body," and risks damaging himself and his relationship to Christ.[53] But, as slaves of God, their role is to glorify God, rather than to live in thrall to their bodily appetites. Their intimate relationship with Christ by means of the Holy Spirit means that to have sex with a prostitute would be tantamount to Christ having sex with a harlot—which is unthinkable.[54]

Given that it was acceptable for Greco-Roman men to use prostitutes, it is perhaps inevitable that such a problem should arise.[55] Various philosophies suggested that sexual freedom was allowable, and it is not unlikely that Corinthian men were attending functions at which prostitutes were available.[56] Paul explains the implications of their new faith: food does not have a polluting effect, but sexual relationships most certainly can. Further, since each individual is part of the body of Christ, the behavior of one will affect the group as a whole (12:12–13).[57] Ultimately, it is a matter of idolatry; attitudes to food and sex tell much about one's allegiances.[58] The community's situation is analogous to that of the people of Israel when they were tempted by the apparent freedom of idolatry (10:7; Exod 32), following their release from Egypt. The lure of the pagan lifestyle may be strong, but they should resist temptation and remember to whom they belong.[59]

53. Pace May, The Body for the Lord," 126, who thinks the relationship is destroyed.

54. Dale B. Martin's claim that sex with a prostitute means copulation of Christ with the evil cosmos (The Corinthian Body, 178) is taking things too far. As May (Body for the Lord, 130) points out, it is not Christ's body, but the believer's, which is permeable.

55. Pace Meeks, The First Urban Christians, 129, who thinks Paul's argument with regard to prostitution is hypothetical.

56. See Paige, "Stoicism, ἐλευθερία and Community at Corinth"; Winter, After Paul Left Corinth, 86–93; cf. Rosner, "Temple Prostitution in 1 Corinthians 6:12–20"; Renate Kirchhoff Die Sünde gegen den eigenten Leib.

57. See Engberg-Pedersen, Cosmology and the Self in the Apostle Paul, 138–71.

58. See Barton, "Food Rules, Sex Rules and the Prohibition of Idolatry."

59. See Meeks, "And Rose up to Play." Cf. Collier, "'That We Might Not Crave Evil.'" On permissiveness as idolatry's primary appeal see Halbertal and Margalit, Idolatry, 24. See further Sandnes, Body and Belly in the Pauline Epistles, 181–216.

Paul may have much to say about the use of prostitutes, but he says nothing about the sexual use of slaves by their owners. In Greco-Roman culture it was taken for granted that masters had sexual access to their slaves, but surely this too would have been considered unacceptable for a believer?[60] Perhaps he does not address the issue here because he does not wish to be thought subversive. Thus, as in the case of Philemon, he does not explicitly challenge long-accepted social hierarchies and practices, but chooses a more subtle approach.[61] From his objection to *porneia* in general we might infer that sex with one's slave would have been out of the question for slaveholders in his churches.[62] Since the female slave is the spiritual equal of the free man (Gal 3:28), she must be out of bounds for sexual exploitation. Further, the fact that in Colossians 3:5, 11—4:1 sexual purity is considered alongside the view that slaves are honorable members of the community, suggests that the practice might have met with disapproval in the Pauline churches.[63]

What of the prostitutes themselves? Sheila Briggs is concerned at Paul's failure to express outrage "at the sexual exploitation of enslaved prostitutes."[64] However, his attitude to those caught up in prostitution is not evident in this passage or any other. In 1 Corinthians, Paul is only concerned with the behavior of men, since they are the ones who have the choice whether or not to use prostitutes. Presumably, given his views regarding sex, if a freewoman who worked as a prostitute joined the community, she would be expected to find other ways of making a living. In this case she would need to be provided for, as alternative forms of employment would be well-nigh impossible to find. However, it is unlikely that a *pornē* would have been able to come to church without her owner's permission, and even if she did, the decision to change her occupation would not be hers to make.[65]

---

60. See Glancy, *Slavery in Early Christianity*; Glancy, "Obstacles to Slaves' Participation in the Corinthian Church"; cf. Marchal, "The Usefulness of an Onesimus."

61. Briggs, "Paul on Bondage and Freedom in Imperial Roman Society." Cf. Osiek, "Slaves, Porneia, and the Limits of Obedience."

62. See Jensen, "Does *Porneia* mean Fornication?."

63. MacDonald, "Slavery, Sexuality and the House Churches."

64. Briggs, "Gender, Slavery and Technology."

65. McGinn, *Prostitution in the Roman World*, 59.

Rahab and Tamar in the New Testament

The genealogy in Matthew 1 cites both Tamar (1:3) and Rahab (1:5) as ancestresses of Jesus, alongside Ruth and Bathsheba. Tamar is mentioned as the mother of Perez and Zerah, Rahab as the mother of Boaz.[66] This is the last we hear of Tamar, but Rahab is mentioned twice more. In Hebrews 11:31 she is cited in a list of people whose faith is approved of by God; a similar commendation appears in James 2:25. The reason for their inclusion in the Matthean genealogy has intrigued scholars. There are many suggestions—that they are gentiles included in Israel, or sinners and special recipients of God's grace, or that they are associated with sexual scandal (thus fore-runners of Mary).[67] In Hebrews 11:31, Rahab appears alongside Abraham, Jacob, and Moses as an exemplar of faithfulness. She is commended for her hospitality to the Hebrew spies, and along with the others on the list, constitutes a warning that those who are faithless will not be spared.[68] The inclusion of a gentile prostitute shows that faith is not restricted to "people of the old covenant."[69] In James 2:25 she is an example of one who is justified by works as well as for her faith (v. 26). She is probably mentioned because of her hospitality to the spies, something that is lacking in the community (vv. 15–16).[70] For all these writers, Tamar and Rahab represent the inclusion of outsiders in God's plan. Their association with prostitution seems to be a reason for their inclusion rather than exclusion—God can use and exalt those whom common opinion and religious authorities might have written off.

66. There is no OT support for the assertion that Rahab is the wife of Salmon and the mother of Boaz. See Guider, *Daughters of Rahab*, 28–36. Josephus describes her as an innkeeper, not a prostitute (Josephus *Antiquities* V). In rabbinic tradition she is said to have married Joshua and become the ancestress of many prophets, including Ezekiel and Jeremiah (e.g., the Talmudic *Tractate Megillah*, 14–15).

67. For a survey of views see Hutchison, "Women, Gentiles, and the Messianic Mission"; see further Levine, "Rahab in the New Testament."

68. Attridge, *The Epistle to the Hebrews*, 345.

69. Gordon, *Hebrews*, 166. See further Eisenbaum, *The Jewish Heroes of Christian History*.

70. Commendation for her hospitality also appears in 1 Clement, which probably influenced the writer of James. See Young, "The Relation of Clement to the Epistle of James."

The Whore of Babylon

In Revelation 17 and 18, as part of his vision of the things that "must take place," John describes "the judgment of the great whore" (17:1), who is said to have committed fornication with the kings of the earth (17:2). She is clothed in rich cloth of purple and scarlet, and wears gold, jewels, and pearls. She holds a golden cup and is drunk on the "abomination and impurities of her fornication" (17:4) and the blood of Christian martyrs (17:6). She sits on a scarlet beast, which is said to be full of blasphemous names and have seven heads and ten horns. Trade has made her rich, kings want to share her power. However, although her clothes and jewelry suggest high status, there is nothing dignified about her.[71] She thinks she is invincible (18:7), but has lost all sense of human decency: she is ugly, blood stained, revolting. She has sunk so low as to be involved in the slave trade (18:13). The woman is the city of Babylon (17:15). The beast is the power behind her success, but the regime must be toppled. Before the beast is destroyed, it will turn on the woman, humiliate her, devour her, and burn her body. There will be great rejoicing (Rev 19:2), and only those who have profited from her will mourn.

Over the centuries, the image of the whore has been variously interpreted, depending on the interests of the reader. It has been understood (*inter alia*) as representing Roman Catholicism, corrupt government, or faulty religion in general.[72] Today, most scholars understand Babylon to represent Rome.[73] Writing in the apocalyptic genre, probably during Domitian's reign (81–96 CE), John aims to encourage believers in Asia Minor, assuring them that the Empire will come to an end and God's rule be established.[74] Together the harlot and the beast represent the oppressive economic and military power of Rome, whose greed and cruelty has corrupted all around her. Following prophetic tradition, the city is depicted as a prostitute—in sharp contrast to the pure and white bride of Christ (19:7–8).[75] Since evil

71. Glancy and Moore, "How Typical a Roman Prostitute is Revelation's 'Great Whore'?"

72. On the history of interpretation see Boxall, "The Many Faces of Babylon the Great"; Kovacs and Rowland, *Revelation*, 177–89.

73. For example, Bauckham, *The Climax of Prophecy*. Cf. the view that the harlot represents Jerusalem in Barker, *The Revelation of Jesus Christ*, 279–301.

74. On apocalyptic literature see Rowland, *The Open Heaven*, 1–70.

75. See Duff, *Who Rides the Beast*, 83–96; Rossing, *The Choice between Two Cities*. On John's use of the prophetic idea of a city as a woman, see Huber, *Like a Bride Adorned*.

and injustice "bear within themselves the seeds of their own destruction," the Empire will be destroyed in the same way as the whore.[76]

Summary

The Old Testament association of prostitution with disorder and impurity finds expression in Paul and the Apocalypse. Paul sees prostitution as a source of corruption, but he also challenges cultural attitudes to male behavior. John takes up the harlotry metaphor to dramatic effect, exposing Rome's corruption, and promising the vindication of God's justice. But the insight found in the Old Testament that cultural rejection of prostitutes is at odds with the mercy and wisdom of God is also found. Rahab and Tamar are honored as part of Jesus' genealogy despite their association with prostitution. For the writer to the Hebrews, Rahab is an exemplar of faith; for James, her works show her loyalty to God.[77]

Jesus overturns the common perception that prostitutes are impure and therefore unacceptable to God, teaching that they, along with other sinners, will go into the kingdom of God before religious leaders. The tradition that Mary Magdalene was a prostitute cannot be substantiated from the texts. The view that the woman who anoints Jesus' feet with her hair is a prostitute may have more substance to it, but this is uncertain. For Jesus, all women are accepted as equals, and purity laws are trumped by the law of love. As members of the outcast and poor, prostitutes are the focus of his message of redemption, but they are loved by God in the same way as any other sinner.

4. A TEACHING OF CONTEMPT?

In Jesus' teaching, there is no suggestion that prostitutes, whether practising or "reformed," deserve any special treatment—either opprobrium or honor. However, some parts of the Bible do seem to suggest otherwise. In several prophecies prostitutes are threatened with humiliating and violent punishment, and the whore of Babylon is destroyed. How should we understand these passages?

---

76. Boxall, *The Revelation of Saint John*, 249.

77. See further Bauckham, *James*, 124–25.

Some feminist readers think they support the view that women in general are to be kept under control, particularly with regard to their sexuality, and promiscuous disobedient women should receive severe penalties.[78] Avaren Ispen's reader-response study with women in prostitution groups has shown that from their perspective, while the story of Rahab is empowering to them, the message of Revelation is "kill the whore." Ipsen sees a link between ideas such as these and the murders of women in prostitution, and suggests that the Bible can and does fuel a mentality that scapegoats the prostitute, and even provides the moral imperative to punish them.[79]

Certainly, there is precedent for thinking these texts offer instruction on the way women should behave. In Ezekiel itself, an early redactor takes the opportunity to urge women to be faithful rather than be like the treacherous harlots (Ezek 23:48).[80] Tertullian used the image of the whore in Revelation to instruct women to dress modestly (*De Cultu Feminarum* II. xii. 2). However, for several reasons, it is misguided to follow these examples.

Firstly, this approach misunderstands the nature of the literature. As we have seen, the aim of both prophetic and apocalyptic literature is to persuade people, at a particular time in history, to be faithful to God. The prophets speak out against apostasy and the injustice that harms the relationship between Yahweh and his people. The Christian Apocalypse encourages first-century believers to persevere in the midst of suffering and to reject the corruption and greed of the surrounding culture. Dramatic scenes and prophetic warnings of the nature we find here, with all their lurid detail, are intended for maximum rhetorical effect, to drive home the message of how seriously God views sin.

Secondly, the language is highly metaphorical, and should not be literalized. Unfortunately, it is possible to lose sight of the fact that these writers are *not really talking about prostitution at all*, either because of the metaphor's emotive power or over-familiarity with the texts.[81] However, as Sandra Schneiders says, "Literalized metaphor is the cancer of the re-

78. See, e.g., Shields, *Circumscribing the Prostitute*, 157; Diamond and O'Connor, "Unfaithful Passions." See also Kim, "Uncovering Her Wickedness"; cf. Weems, *Battered Love*; Pippin, *Death and Desire*.

79. Ipsen, *Sex Working in the Bible*, 177–83.

80. Verses 36–49 are probably editorial additions. See Zimmerli, *Ezekiel 1*, 492. See further Mein, "Ezekiel's Women in Christian Interpretation."

81. Fiorenza, *The Power of the Word*, 140–47. On the nature of metaphor see Paul, "The Book of Revelation"; Ricoeur, *The Rule of Metaphor*. On the use of metaphor in the prophetic literature see O'Brien, *Challenging Prophetic Metaphor*.

ligious imagination, powerfully and pathologically at work."[82] It can easily lead to a false inference—that because God is said to deal violently with these (metaphorical) women, then so should we with real, flesh-and-blood women. Literalized interpretation of the harlot image can lead to, if not the dehumanizing and brutalizing of those caught up in prostitution, an attitude that supports their stigmatization and rejection—on the grounds that this is God's will.[83]

Thirdly, the prophets' use of the harlot metaphor is deeply ironic. The challenges to prevailing cultural norms that we noted in the Tamar and Rahab narratives are also found here, but are presented even more subtly. In Ezekiel, at a surface level, the focus seems to be on the sin of the prostitute as an illustration of the worst that sin can be, but the prurient imaginings cleverly disguise the fact that the real target of the polemic is the powerful men who are causing the nation to apostatize. When Jerusalem and Samaria are depicted as prostitutes, these leaders are being feminized and insulted. Similarly, for much of the time in Hosea, Yahweh seems to be a cruel and vengeful God whose threatened punishment of the prostitute is extreme. However, it turns out that the idea that God would treat someone in this cruel and humiliating way has more to do with the human imagination than the truth about God's compassion and mercy. As Carolyn Sharp notes,

> The true God is other than the abusive god who would have killed her; hence, Israel must learn to cherish this woman who apparently represented apostasy but whose orphaned children are yet loved and protected by God. In reflecting on this mystery, the community of Israel learns to privilege not judgement but love and forgiveness in its theology.[84]

Lastly, the use of the metaphor reflects cultural and moral norms that are different to ours. As Elizabeth Schüssler Fiorenza writes with regard to Revelation, while the language and symbolic universe "fit" its historical-critical situation, it will not necessarily cohere with ours.[85] The power of the

---

82. Schneiders, *Revelatory Text*, 30.

83. Bushman et al., "When God Sanctions Killing." By the same token, some feminist readers literalize the metaphor in order to emphasize the degradation of women in these texts and risk undermining engagement with the prophets' concerns about social justice. See Carson, "The Harlot, the Beast, and the Sex Trafficker."

84. Sharp, *Irony and Meaning in the Hebrew Bible*, 122–23. See further Sherwood, *The Prostitute and the Prophet*.

85. Fiorenza, *The Book of Revelation*, 199.

metaphor for first-century readers stems from its resonances of impurity in Jewish tradition. It exploits the deep-seated fears that led to the polarity of cult and prostitution. The violent punishments of the prostitutes in Ezekiel and Hosea reflect ancient Near Eastern practices and beliefs.[86] But these norms are not ours, and nor should they be—not least in the light of the teachings of Jesus. The harsh treatment of these metaphorical harlots does not mean that we should think prostitutes deserving of humiliating punishment any more than we should believe that because Abraham had slaves, we should too.[87]

For these reasons, these passages cannot be used to support the idea that prostitutes should be subject to harsh punishment. Indeed, despite appearances to the contrary, they belong to that strand in Scripture that undermines prevailing cultural values and subverts the norms that keep people in power, pointing to God's demand for justice. For they are not about prostitutes at all, but about a righteous God who cannot stand the behavior of those who profess to be His own but who are really turning away from Him.

5. PROSTITUTION AND SEX TRAFFICKING IN CANONICAL PERSPECTIVE

Throughout Scripture, the sale and purchase of sex is considered an undesirable element in society, associated with violence, corruption, and idolatry. At the same time, the Bible records and reflects the double standards, fascination, and revulsion that have characterized discussions of prostitution throughout history. Readers, therefore, have a responsibility to work to discern the ethos of redemption and love over against those strands that reflect cultural and religious prejudices and fears. Powerful voices might lead us to think that the solution to the problem of prostitution is to target the women involved.[88] In fact, however, there is a "redemptive impulse" with regard to individuals. The stigmatizing of women in prostitution is continually undermined and subverted—subtly in narratives such as Tamar and Rahab, covertly in the prophetic literature, and openly in the ministry of Jesus. Once again, those thought to be shameful by society, are honorable in God's sight.

86. See Magdalene, "Ancient NE Treaty-Curses and the Ultimate Texts of Terror."

87. Sanderson, "Nahum."

88. For this view see Davies, "On Prostitution."

The biblical literature also reflects the complex nature of prostitution. In both Testaments there is a compassionate awareness that women may have to resort to prostitution in order to survive, and a shrewd acknowledgement that those who do so might be exploiting men as much as men are exploiting them. Remarkably, too, men have a responsibility not to collude in the sexual objectification of women. The idea of the repentant prostitute as particularly close to God cannot be substantiated from the biblical texts, and contrary to popular understanding, the notion of a Madonna-whore dichotomy, which has been so influential in Christian history, is based on a faulty understanding of the texts. In fact, Jesus is much less interested in prostitution than Christian tradition might lead us to expect. He is far more concerned with the religious hypocrisy that condemns and rejects those considered to be sinners. The redemptive impulse applies to all those who are considered to be outcasts by religious authorities and society as a whole.

Our study suggests that prostitution should not be considered a legitimate "career choice," not because it is inherently sinful, but because its view of human sexuality is based on a false dichotomy between the physical and the spiritual, and that it can be harmful for the individuals involved. However, to view those caught up in prostitution as sinners is misguided, and the church should beware of adding to the stigma that causes so much suffering, at the same time exposing and challenging the double standards regarding male and female sexual behavior that help to perpetuate it.

As far as current policy-making discussions are concerned, our study suggests that legalization of the sex industry would not be in line with the canonical ethos, but that decriminalization of those caught up in prostitution should be considered, not least so that they can have hope of a different way of making a living. The current shift of focus away from those working in prostitution to "male demand" seems consistent with the biblical teaching on equality between men and women and the call for men to take responsibility of their sexual behavior. Those who coerce others into prostitution should, of course, be considered criminal, and brought to justice.

As the church considers its response to sex trafficking, we do well to examine ourselves, and realize that it is easy to allow our own attitudes to sexuality and gender to drive our response. Most often, these attitudes stem from our cultural and religious contexts, whose values, prejudices, and assumptions we unconsciously absorb. But as we saw with regard to slavery, the canon of Scripture continually challenges these assumptions, undercutting our attempts to preserve them when they lead to the oppression of those who are weakest (or considered to be weakest) in society. We should be careful that the powerful associations of sin and shame that have characterized human reactions to prostitution from the biblical period right up to the present day, lead us either to ignore the existence of sex trafficking altogether, or place so much emphasis on it that we compromise our response to contemporary slavery as whole.

CHAPTER 6

The Bible
and
Contemporary Slavery

1. SUMMARY OF THE ARGUMENT

The principal aim of this book has been to ask what the Bible has to say to us about modern-day slavery. However, at the outset I suggested that in order to do this with integrity, two questions had to be addressed by way of preparatory groundwork. The first question had to do with hermeneutics, and the second to do with Christian attitudes to prostitution. Concerning the Bible, we noted that there is a fundamental problem with regard to its use in the discussion of human trafficking. While the biblical worldview considers slavery to be the norm, modern society sees it as morally unacceptable. However, since all major Christian traditions understand the Bible to be normative for faith and practice, to ignore this anomaly is at best lazy and at worst dishonest. We cannot ignore it, so we must try to find a way through it.

With regard to prostitution, we noted that views of prostitution directly affect how sex trafficking is understood and tackled. However, a simplistic association of prostitution with sin in the minds of many Christians, along with cultural and religious attitudes that often render it a taboo subject, can inhibit balanced discussion. There is therefore a need, not only to be aware of the issues involved, but also to recognize that we may have presuppositions and prejudices that might compromise our response to the issue.

Our first task was to address the problem of the difference between the worldview of the Bible and our own with regard to slavery. How are we to bridge the hermeneutical gap? Noting that there is historical precedent on which to draw, we considered the role of the Bible in the abolitionist campaign. We saw that the Quakers, who were so influential in early anti-slavery thinking, prized ideals of love, freedom, and equality, whose essence they saw encapsulated in the principle of the law of love. Pro-slavery advocates, on the other hand, found legal endorsement of slavery in the Bible, and maintained that it was ordained by God. As the campaign progressed, their rule-based, literalist approach came to be seen as self-seeking, lacking in love, and as a hindrance to the alleviation of injustice and suffering. On the other hand, anti-slavery campaigners, as well as slaves themselves, found that biblical narratives of redemption and *agape* love gave courage and impetus to combat slavery as antipathetic to the ethos of the gospel. A hermeneutic of empathy and compassion triumphed over prescriptive literalism.

With this in mind, we then turned to the biblical material itself to see if and how it can inform contemporary anti-slavery work. First of all, we tested the abolitionist hermeneutical approach: does it still stand up—two centuries later? Adopting a canonical view of Scripture, and drawing on modern developments in biblical studies, we conducted a survey of major biblical texts dealing with slavery and found that while many passages do uphold slaveholding, there is a "redemptive impulse" that overrides these. At times, this can be hard to discern, especially in those passages that reflect Israel's and the church's attempts to grasp what it means to live as the people of God. Nevertheless, values of equality, human dignity, and freedom are to be traced throughout both Testaments, albeit often articulated imperfectly. They are conveyed with particular clarity and beauty in narratives—for example in the Joseph and exodus stories. Above all, they are central to the story and message of Christ, the slave-king who comes to redeem his people.

The redemptive impulse that permeates Scripture can still inspire and inform Christian efforts to counter the injustice of slavery. Human trafficking compromises the dignity of victims, perpetrators, and those who buy the services they provide. In prophetic fashion, Christians can speak out against the greed, exploitation, and injustice which perpetuates slavery, identify with those who are oppressed, care for victims, and work for the wellbeing of those at risk of exploitation.[1] The call to follow Jesus' example of sacrificial identification with those whom society rejects forms the basis of anti-slavery work today.

But what about the sex industry, into which so many are trafficked, and the difficult moral questions that pertain to it? Chapter 4 set out to demonstrate the complexity of the issues, and to help readers to identify their own presuppositions with regard to adult prostitution in preparation for looking at the biblical texts. The ambivalence and double standards that have tended to characterize attitudes to prostitution, in both secular society and the church, were highlighted and explored. We also highlighted the sharp division between those who think that prostitution is an acceptable occupation (if not a service to society) and those who do not, and between those who think it fundamentally exploitative and those who do not, noting that our response to these questions has a direct bearing on how we think sex trafficking should be tackled.

Our next task therefore was to turn to the biblical texts themselves to see if they can help us address some of these questions. Bearing in mind the ambivalence and even cruelty that has tended to characterize the church's dealings with those caught up in prostitution, we again drew on the lessons learned from the abolitionist hermeneutic, resisting the temptation to look solely for rules and prescription, and seeking an ethos within Scripture that is congruent with the law of love. Our survey suggested a sense throughout Scripture that prostitution is an undesirable element in society, because of its associations with idolatry and disorder. The development of the harlotry metaphor to speak of apostasy heightens a sense of taboo. While prostitutes are shunned, however, there are strands in the documents that recognize that this might be a blinkered and even unjust reaction, and this challenge to the common cultural and religious view continues in the New Testament. True, Paul sees prostitution as a source of corruption, and the fear and revulsion associated with it is exploited again in the apocalyptic vision of the whore of Babylon in the book of Revelation. However, Jesus speaks of prostitutes as being among the outcast and poor, and while the religious authorities reject them, these are the very groups who are the focus of his redeeming ministry. Moreover, in a rather remarkable development, Paul

1. For a similar view of the place of the Bible in effecting social reform see Mott, *Biblical Ethics and Social Change.*

insists that men should be accountable for their behavior. To purchase sex is incompatible with being a follower of Christ.

Thus, the biblical literature supports the view that Christians should work towards the eradication of prostitution—but without condemning prostitutes themselves. Indeed, we should be very careful about branding people who are caught up in prostitution as sinners—for, like Tamar and Rahab, they may well turn out to be more righteous than those who seem to adhere to cultural and religious norms. Nor can we make blanket statements as to whether prostitution is inherently exploitative: sometimes it is, and sometimes it is not. For some who find themselves in great poverty or need, prostitution may be the only option. The taboos and prejudices that often accompany discussion of the topic and the ambivalence that has been characteristic of the church's approach to tackling the problem are largely the product of human fear and prejudice rather than congruent with the love of God. Traditional ideas that women in prostitution were prominent in Jesus ministry and thus especially dear to God do not have their basis in the biblical literature, but are the product of medieval notions of idealized womanhood.

Thus, we conclude that instead of adding to the burden of those who are or have been exploited and abused, the church should be looking for ways to prevent that exploitation in the first place—drawing attention to the customers' role in perpetuating prostitution, refusing to collude in systems of corruption, greed, and inequality, which render people vulnerable, and calling to account those who exploit, abuse, and traffic others into prostitution. For many Christians throughout the world this will require a radical change in their thinking, but perhaps, in this way, we can begin to address the evil that is sex trafficking.

2. PRACTICAL IMPLICATIONS

The biblical ethos of redemption and freedom has profound implications for a Christian response to human trafficking. Theologically, the canon of Scripture provides us with a view of God and his dealings with humanity that informs how we live our lives as a community of believers, and the values that form the basis of our dealings with each other. Within the church itself, it is first a matter of realizing our own identity. Christians should constantly be aware of themselves as people redeemed by God, and should nurture an ethos of justice and equality, and mutual service. The dignity of all humanity is a fundamental value, and we must constantly work against any tendency within our ranks to consider others as means rather than ends in themselves. We should refuse to collude with the corrupt and greedy who seek to exploit others, and recognize our own susceptibility to the temptation to seek out power and wealth.

But an ethic of love and redemption means also that the church must look beyond itself, and reach out to others. Just as Jesus, the slave-king, identified with the oppressed and exploited, and challenged views that contributed to their exploitation, so should Christians. The redemption narrative urges us not to retreat from the world, protecting ourselves from what we perceive as morally dangerous, but to identify with the outcast and poor and include them in the community of believers. This means that we need to be involved with the lives of real people—not avoiding them as unsuitable company. Rules, principles, and ideas are most easily maintained in abstraction. If we are out in the world and mixing with others, rather than retreating into a comfortable enclave, we might begin to see lives changed.

At grass-roots level, therefore, Christians can become involved in practical work—rescuing and caring for victims of traffickers, welcoming them into the church, and enabling their reintegration into society. This can take the form of rehabilitation centres, safe houses, and social and psychological care appropriate to the culture. Just as important is prevention work: raising awareness of the problem amongst the general public. We can educate those at risk to have a healthy view of their intrinsic worth and human dignity and to be able to recognize the mindset that sees others as inferior to themselves or as objects to be bought and sold.[2] So too, at policy-making levels, Christians can actively support these practical efforts. They can also work to alleviate the poverty that drives many into slavery in the first place—enabling and providing non-exploitative employment in which profits are shared responsibly, buying ethically-sourced goods, and speaking out against the oppression, corruption, and greed that feeds upon the vulnerability of others.

With regard to the particular problem of sex trafficking, the Bible warns us against stigmatizing those not considered respectable, and urges that we contest cultural and religious prejudices that marginalize or exclude some from our communities of faith. As a first step, attitudes to women and children (especially girls) are crucial in this regard. Any view that sees them as inferior and unworthy of education must be challenged, as should any

2. See Bales, *Ending Slavery*.

form of sexual objectification. Stereotypical notions of women in prostitution as sinners will only hinder appropriate Christian responses.[3] And, as Lia Claire Scholl notes, the refusal to marginalize applies to men and transgendered people who work in prostitution too.[4] The Gospels record Jesus as cutting through cultural and religious taboos, and welcoming all those considered to be outcasts by religious authorities. At the very least, then, the church should not be complicit in the shaming of those involved in prostitution—there are plenty of others who will do that, including pimps and traffickers, who use it as a powerful tool to destroy their victims' sense of self-worth.

Our study suggests that Christians cannot support the view that the legalization of prostitution should be pursued in order to decrease the numbers trafficked into the sex trade. Certainly, as we have noted, some may have no alternative for the support of their families. However, for most people, working in prostitution is likely to be harmful—both psychologically and physically, not least because of the risk of violence from customers and pimps. The image of the harlot in the prophets and the whore of Babylon may be distasteful to us, but the linking of prostitution with rape, sexual humiliation, and violence, reflects the harsh reality of the lives of many who are caught up in prostitution today. On the other hand, we should seriously consider decriminalization of those who work as prostitutes, to enable them to find other work.[5]

Double standards should be exposed, and the conventional pattern of turning a blind eye to male behavior challenged—both within the church and in society as a whole. Paul's words on the subject may not go as far as many today would like, but we can build upon the work that he began. Current attempts to reduce prostitution and sex trafficking by tackling demand and criminalizing those who buy sex are congruent with this acknowledgment of male responsibility. Moreover, transient impersonal sexual relationships are contrary to the biblical understanding of the nature of human sexuality. Therefore, the sex industry, which relies on the objectification of women and children for precisely this purpose, cannot be seen simply as another aspect of the entertainment business, but as exploitative and unhealthy.

3. Wu, "Women on the Boundary."

4. Scholl, I (Heart) Sex Workers.

5. Brock and Thistlethwaite, Casting Stones, 261. For further discussion of how Christians can respond to sex trafficking see Miles and Crawford, Stopping the Traffick.

3. SCRIPTURE, SLAVERY, AND HERMENEUTICS

Any doubts as to the relevance of the Bible for discussions of contemporary human trafficking should, I hope, have been dispelled. Granted, the difference between its worldview and our own must be acknowledged, but the contention of this book has been that the central narrative of God's dealings with his people provides a hermeneutical key that allows us to look beyond the cultural settings represented within it and find the timeless ethos and values that are the basis for ethics in any age. Of course, there is nothing new in this. Jesus' teaching, and that of the Old Testament prophets, has always encouraged people to work against evil, both at a structural level and at the level of individual sin and idolatry. Biblical stories such as the exodus have long inspired people to rise up against tyranny and oppression.[6] The exodus narrative gave American slaves hope and inspired courageous rebellion against injustice.[7] It motivates black people in their continued struggle against oppression, and is of central importance for liberation theologians working amongst the poor in South America and throughout the world.[8] The same is true today, despite the misgivings of some that advances in biblical scholarship have rendered these readings spurious and invalid. The redemptive impulse of Scripture continues to provide the foundation for a Christian response to human trafficking in all its contemporary forms.

However, it is not enough simply to assert the Bible's continued relevance for anti-trafficking work today, or even to show why this is so, as we have attempted to do here. If nothing else, this study has shown that we must also be aware of *how* the Bible is read and used. In other words, we have to be *ethical* readers. As the history of the abolitionist debate shows, it is tempting to refer to the Bible to support one's own cause, and to use it to promote one's own interests at the expense of others.' While most Christians would not knowingly do this, it is possible to do so unconsciously. Many Southern slave-holders genuinely believed that the Bible supported and even commanded the keeping of slaves. Of course, they were influenced by their own times and cultures, and it is easy for us to look back and be critical. Nevertheless, their story alerts us to the danger of faulty interpretation. But how can we avoid this? How can we ensure an ethical

6. Waltzer, *Exodus and Revolution.*

7. Kirk-Duggan, "Let My People Go!"

8. On black theology see further Antonio, "Black Theology"; Song, "The Black Experience of the Exodus." On liberation theology see, for example, Croatto, *Exodus;* Nogueira, "Exodus in Latin America."

use of the Bible, and not a selfish manipulation of it for our own ends? Some suggestions may be made.

Firstly, readers have a responsibility to be aware, as far as is possible, of their own assumptions and agendas. The story of the slaveholders' use of the Bible demonstrates how easily Scripture can be used to further one's own cause, and even to oppress others.[9] As the history of Christian attitudes towards women in prostitution has shown, this is by no means an isolated case. There are therefore important questions to ask. For example, what in our worldview and culture might hinder us from working in a redemptive loving spirit? Are we seeking to further our own ends rather than the well-being of others?

Second, it is important to resist the temptation to reduce the Bible to a book of rules, principles, and data.[10] While such an approach might seem the most natural and most faithful to the text, it fails to do justice to the richness and depth of the biblical literature, and can ultimately be self-seeking and destructive, blinding us to the overall ethos of the Christ story. To look for timeless, universalizable prescription in Old Testament law and New Testament paraenesis is to misunderstand their nature and purpose. These passages must be understood (as far as is possible) in their historical context and in the light of the central message of the gospel—that Jesus comes to set the captives free. This expresses a fundamental ethos of freedom, justice, and human dignity, which is presented in many different ways throughout the canon and which can still speak to us today.

A literalistic approach to Scripture tends towards a proof-texting mentality that is not only hard to gainsay but also runs the risk of silencing the compassion and empathy that is at the heart of the biblical ethos. This does not mean that rules and principles are completely invalid—there are times when this kind of approach is helpful and appropriate. It does mean, however, that we should not be tempted into universalizing them or into reducing Christian life to a matter of law. Prescriptive law has its place, but there is much more to Christian life than this.[11] The study of how the abolitionists worked with the Bible suggests that when it comes to social change, a prescriptive approach is inadequate, even counterproductive. The church

---

9. Fiorenza, *Rhetoric and Ethic*; Patte, *Ethics of Biblical Interpretation*; Siebert, *The Violence of Scripture*; Barton, "The Bible in Black Theology"; Johnson, "The Bible, Slavery and the Problem of Authority."

10. Jantzen, *Old Testament Ethics*.

11. Wenham, "The Gap between Law and Ethics in the Bible."

is more likely to be effective in the world if it seeks to be a community of followers of Jesus Christ than if it tries to impose rules on society.[12] It is therefore much more fruitful to look for and act in accordance with the redemptive ethos and values that pervade the canon of Scripture and are exemplified in the life and teaching of Jesus.[13] Nor need this preclude rigorous exegesis. The fact that the canon of Scripture contains various types of literature that demand different hermeneutical strategies for interpretation means that intuitive and critical approaches to Scripture should not be considered mutually exclusive, but necessarily complementary for balanced biblical study.[14]

Third, we must accept that our understanding of Scripture will always be inadequate and imperfect, simply because our understanding of the Bible will always be informed by our own local circumstances and influences.[15] The Princeton evangelicals were seduced by the idea of scientific certainty, and their work became tarnished as a result. Rather, following the example of the Old Testament writers, we profit from continually revising our understanding of what it means to be the people of God, which in turn leads to serving others in ways appropriate to time and culture. As Walter Brueggemann says, God is a "restless agent of social newness."[16] Similarly, Christian discipleship is never static, it never assumes that it understands fully, or has nothing else to learn. But the fact that Jesus is still present through the Holy Spirit means that we too must continually be reassessing what it means to be his followers, and readers of Scripture, in any given age.

Lastly, continuing work needs to be done in the academy and the church to help readers discern and recognize the various voices represented in Scripture.[17] There is a constant risk of mistaking the human voices of culture and religion for those that point us towards the will of God. As we have seen, these voices, which can represent the powerful in society, can be very strong indeed. However, failure to hear the sometimes more muted,

---

12. Hauerwas, *The Peaceable Kingdom*; Ogletree, *The Use of the Bible in Christian Ethics*, 205.

13. The bibliography for this approach to biblical ethics is growing. See for example, Cahill, "The New Testament and Ethics"; Verhey, *Remembering Jesus*; Burridge, *Imitating Jesus*.

14. See Kahl, "Growing Together," who calls for the collaboration of "intuitive" and "critical readers" to work towards more balanced biblical interpretation.

15. For this line of thinking see, for example, Adam, "Twisting to Destruction."

16. Brueggemann, *Theology of the Old Testament*, 178.

17. See Thiselton, "Canon, Community, and Theological Construction."

subversive voice of love can risk compromising the church's understanding of its duty to work towards social justice and the care of God's creation.[18] One way of helping us with this would be to conduct studies of Scripture with groups of people familiar with and vulnerable to trafficking. Ipsen's reader-response study was carried out with female prostitutes' rights activists, and it helps us to hear how they respond to the Bible. We need to hear from other groups too, in order to gain an understanding of how different people read the Scriptures. As we saw with regard to slavery, the slaves themselves took a very different view of the Bible from their masters. We constantly need to have our hermeneutic challenged and tested in the light of the redeeming impulse of the gospel.

4. CONCLUSION

In this book, I have not set out to provide a comprehensive study of all that the Bible has to say about human trafficking. Instead, I have tried to introduce the subject, in the hope that it will stimulate further discussion and study, and above all, action. The Bible is our starting point in all this. But rather than looking to it to provide answers for any and every situation, I have suggested here that we can look for a biblical *ethos*, and some guidance as to how that ethos plays out in practice. Hermeneutical settings and worldviews will change, and theorists and activists will need to be further informed on the political, cultural, and social settings in which they are working. How we react to the human tendency to enslave and exploit will require constant revision, but the central narrative of Scripture means that the imperative for Christians to work towards freedom for slaves remains constant. In the light of the work of God's redeeming work amongst his people, throughout history and above all in the person and work of Jesus Christ, it goes without saying that Christians should work for the freedom of others in this world. As Bruce Birch says, "God does not liberate without also calling us to the vocation of liberation. God does not confront the powers without calling us to confront them in God's name."[19]

Of course, efforts towards freedom will not be welcomed by everyone. There will be opposition—and not only from traffickers and others who stand to gain from their activities. Some victims of trafficking may resist the idea of such a change to their lives altogether. They may have known

18. See Brueggemann, *Truth Speaks to Power*.

19. Birch, *Let Justice Roll Down*, 127–28.

nothing else, and find it very difficult to adapt to a life outside slavery. As Pinchas Lapide reminds us, it took forty years for Israel's slave mentality to go.[20] Others, such as those for whom bonded labor may seem to be the only option, may resent the attempts to remove their only means of survival. Nevertheless, the Christian Scriptures suggest that there is a responsibility to see ourselves as part of its redemptive impulse and, with sensitivity and courage, bring its power into the lives of people today.

In comparison with the eighteenth- and nineteenth-century abolitionists' campaign against a legalized system of slavery, ours is a different, far more complex task. Migration and economic policies at national and international level play a crucial role in the reduction of human trafficking. So too, social systems (for example, the caste system of India) that perpetuate slavery, corrupt governments and police systems that tolerate and support criminal gangs, materialism that turns a blind eye to the suffering of those who produce goods in exploitative situations, toleration of sexual exploitation, and business that looks to profit at the expense of the poor, all need to be tackled. In all these areas, and more, the church can make its voice heard, confident that the Bible can continue to inspire the fight against slavery in ever new ways.

Throughout this study, our attention has been repeatedly drawn to the fact that, for Christians, anti-slavery work must begin with self-examination. It is easy to say that we are committed to ending human trafficking, but it is just as easy to believe that the responsibility lies with others—those who are especially "called" to do the work. However, we are all called to have the mind of Christ, who identified with the weak and vulnerable in society, rather than live with ambitions of power, wealth, and status. This requires that we look at our attitudes to gender, race, and social class. For many Christians living in the developed world, it will certainly require an examination of our attitudes towards money—how we earn it, spend it, and invest it—and our relationship to business and profit. To obey this calling entails risk and sacrifice. Moreover, while the church has a prophetic voice in a world in which people are in danger of being trafficked and becoming traffickers, we must also constantly guard against the hypocrisy and self-righteousness that Jesus so often condemned. Lastly, while there may be many doctrinal and cultural differences among Christians, there can surely be no disagreement that we must work together to fulfill the demand of the gospel and set the captives free.

20. Lapide, "Exodus in the Jewish Tradition."

Bibliography

Aageson, James. *Paul, the Pastoral Epistles and the Early Church*. Peabody, MA: Hendrickson, 2008.

Aasgaard, Reidar. "'Brotherly Advice': Christian Siblingship and New Testament Paraenesis." In *Early Christian Paraenesis in Context*, edited by James Starr & Troels Engberg-Pedersen, 237–66. Berlin: de Gruyter, 2004.

Abma, R. *Bonds of Love: Methodic Studies of Prophetic Texts with Marriage Imagery (Isaiah 50:1–3 and 54:1–10, Hosea 1–3, Jeremiah 2–3)*. Assen, Netherlands: Van Gorcum, 1999.

Acton, William. *Prostitution, Considered in Its Moral, Social and Sanitary Aspects in London and Other Large Cities, with Proposals for the Mitigation and Prevention of Its Attendant Evils*. London: Churchill, 1857.

Adam, A. K. M. "Twisting to Destruction: A Memorandum on the Ethics of Interpretation." In *Faithful Interpretation: Reading the Bible in a Postmodern World*, 57–65. Minneapolis: Fortress, 2006.

Affleck, Thomas. *"Duties of Overseers" Cotton Plantation Record and Account Book No 3 suitable for a Force of 120 Hands, or under*. 7th ed. New Orleans: Norman, 1857. Reprinted in *Slavery*, edited by Stanley Engerman et al., 242–45. Oxford: Oxford University Press, 2001.

Agustin, Laura Maria. *Sex at the Margins: Migration, Labour Markets and the Rescue Industry*. London: Zed, 2007.

Agutter, William. "The Abolition of the Slave Trade considered in a Religious Point of View. A Sermon Preached before the Corporation of the city of Oxford, at St Martin's Church, on Sunday February 3rd 1788 by William Agutter M.A. of St Mary Magdalen College." Reprinted in Bodleian Library, *The Slave Trade Debate*, 272–84. Oxford, Bodlean Library, 2007.

Allison, Dale C. *The New Moses: A Matthean Typology*. Minneapolis: Augsburg Fortress, 1993.

Amit, Yaira. "The Jubilee Law—An Attempt at Instituting Social Justice." In *Justice and Righteousness: Biblical Themes and their Influence*, edited by Henning Graf Reventlow & Yair Hoffman, 47–59. Sheffield, UK: Sheffield Academic Press, 2009.

Anderson, Bernard W. "Exodus and Covenant in Second Isaiah and Prophetic Tradition." In *Magnalia Dei: The Mighty Acts of God: Essays on the Bible and Archaeology in Memory of G. Ernest Wright*, edited by F. M. Moore et al., 339–60. New York: Doubleday, 1976.

Anderson, Cheryl B. *Women, Ideology and Violence: Critical Theory and the Construction of Gender in the Book of the Covenant and the Deuteronomic Law.* London: T. & T. Clark, 2004.

Anstey, Roger T. *The Atlantic Slave Trade and British Abolition 1760–1810.* London: Macmillan, 1975.

———. "Religion and British Slave Emancipation." In *The Abolition of the Slave Trade: Origins and Effects in Europe, Africa and the Americas*, edited by David Eltis and James Walvin, 37–61. Madison, WI: University of Wisconsin Press, 1981.

Antonio, Edward P. "Black Theology." In *The Cambridge Companion to Liberation Theology*, 2nd ed., edited by Christopher Rowland, 79–104. Cambridge: Cambridge University Press, 2007.

Attridge, Harold W. "'Don't Be Touching Me': Recent Feminist Scholarship on Mary Magdalene." In *A Feminist Companion to John*, vol. 2, edited by Amy-Jill Levine with Marianne Bickenstaff, 140–67. Sheffield, UK: Sheffield Academic Press, 2003.

———. *The Epistle to the Hebrews.* Philadelphia: Fortress, 1989.

Avalos, Hector. *Slavery, Abolitionism and the Ethics of Biblical Studies.* Sheffield, UK: Sheffield Phoenix, 2011.

Baker, David L. *Tight Fists or Open Hands? Wealth and Poverty in Old Testament Law.* Grand Rapids: Eerdmans, 2007.

Bal, Mieke. *Death and Dissymmetry: The Politics of Coherence in the Book of Judges.* Chicago: University of Chicago Press, 1988.

Balch, David L. *Let Wives Be Submissive: The Domestic Code in 1 Peter.* Atlanta: Scholars, 1981.

Bales, K. *Disposable People: New Slavery in the Global Economy.* Rev. ed. Berkeley: University of California Press, 2000

———. *Ending Slavery: How We Free Today's Slaves.* Berkeley: University of California Press, 2007.

———. "How We Will End Slavery in the Twenty-first Century." In *Slavery Now and Then*, edited by Danny Smith, 29–43. Eastbourne, UK: Kingsway, 2007.

———. *Understanding Global Slavery: A Reader.* Berkeley: University of California Press, 2005.

Barclay, John M. G. "Am I not a Man and a Brother? The Bible and the British Anti-Slavery Debate." *ExpTim* 119 (2007) 3–14.

———. "Paul, Philemon and the Dilemma of Christian Slave Ownership." *NTS* 37 (1991) 161–86.

Barker, Margaret. *The Revelation of Jesus Christ: Which God gave to Him to Show to His Servants What Must Soon Take Place (Revelation 1:1).* Edinburgh: T. & T. Clark, 2000.

Barnes, Albert. *An Inquiry into the Scriptural Views of Slavery.* Philadelphia: Parry & McMillan, 1857.

Barr, James. *The Concept of Biblical Theology: An Old Testament Perspective.* Minneapolis: Fortress, 1999.

Barry, Kathleen. *The Prostitution of Sexuality: The Global Exploitation of Women.* New York: New York University Press, 1995.

Bartchy, S.S. *ΜΑΛΛΟΝ ΧΡΕΣΑΙ: First Century Slavery and the Interpretation of 1 Cor. 7.21.* Missoula: University of Montana, 1973.

Barthe, Markus, and Helmut Blanke. *The Letter to Philemon: A New Translation with Notes and Commentary*. Grand Rapids: Eerdmans, 2000.

Bartholomew, Craig G. "How has the Bible Been Used Ethically?" In *A Royal Priesthood? The Use of the Bible Ethically and Politically. A Dialogue with Oliver O'Donovan*, edited by Craig Bartholomew et al., 12–19. Scripture and Hermeneutics, vol. 3. Carlisle, UK: Paternoster, 2002.

Bartley, Paula. *Prostitution: Prevention and Reform in England 1860–1914*. London: Routledge, 2000.

Barton, John. "The Basis of Ethics in the Hebrew Bible." *Semeia* 66 (1994) 11–22.

———. *People of the Book? The Authority of the Bible in Christianity*. London: SPCK, 1993

Barton, Mukti. "The Bible in Black Theology." *Black Theology* 9 (2011) 57–76.

Barton, Stephen C. "Food Rules, Sex Rules and the Prohibition of Idolatry." In *Idolatry: False Worship in the Bible, Early Judaism and Christianity*, edited by Stephen C. Barton, 141–62. London: T. & T. Clark, 2007.

Bassiouni, M. Cherif. "Enslavement as an International Crime" *New York University Journal of Law and Politics* 23 (1991) 445–517.

Bauckham, Richard. *The Bible in Politics*. London: SPCK, 1989.

———. *The Climax of Prophecy: Studies in the Book of Revelation*. Edinburgh: T. & T. Clark, 1993.

———. *James: Wisdom of James, Disciple of Jesus the Sage*. London: Routledge, 1999.

Bebbington, David. *Evangelicalism in Modern Britain: A History from the 1730s to the 1980s*. Grand Rapids: Baker, 1989.

Beirne, Margaret, M. *Women and Men in the Fourth Gospel: A Genuine Discipleship of Equals*. Sheffield, UK: Sheffield Academic Press, 2003.

Bell, Michael. *Sentimentalism, Ethics and the Culture of Feeling*. Basingstoke, UK: Palgrave, 2000.

Bennett, Harold V. *Injustice Made Legal: Deuteronomic Law and the Plight of Widows, Strangers, and Orphans in Ancient Israel*. Grand Rapids: Eerdmans, 2002.

Bernheimer, Charles. *Figures of Ill-Repute: Representing Prostitution in Nineteenth Century France*. Durham, NC: Duke University Press, 1989.

Bernstein, Elizabeth. *Temporarily Yours: Intimacy, Authenticity and the Commerce of Sex*. Chicago: University of Chicago Press, 2007.

Berquist, Jon L. *Controlling Corporeality: The Body and the Household in Ancient Israel*. New Brunswick: Rutgers University Press, 2002.

Bindman, Jo, with Jo Doexema. *Redefining Prostitution as Sex Work on the International Agenda*. London: AntiSlavery International, 2007.

Birch Bruce C. "Divine Character and the Formation of Moral Community in the Book of Exodus." In *The Bible in Ethics: The Second Sheffield Colloquium*, edited by John W. Rogerson et al., 119–35. Sheffield, UK: Sheffield Academic Press, 1995.

———. *Let Justice Roll Down: The Old Testament, Ethics and the Christian Life*. Louisville: Westminster John Knox, 1991.

Birch, Bruce C.. and Larry L. Rasmussen. *Bible and Ethics in the Christian Life*. Rev. ed. Minneapolis: Fortress, 1989.

Bird, Phyllis A. "The End of the Male Cult Prostitute: A Literary-Historical and Social Analysis of Hebrew QĀDĒŠ-QĔDĒŠîM." In *Congress Volume: Cambridge 1995*, edited by John A. Emerton, 37–80. VTSupp vol. 66. Leiden: Brill, 1997.

——. "'To Play the Harlot': An Enquiry into an Old Testament Metaphor." In *Missing Persons and Mistaken Identities: Women and Gender in Ancient Israel*, 219–38. Minneapolis: Augsburg Fortress, 1997.

Bland, Lucy. *Banishing the Beast: Feminism, Sex and Morality*. London: Tauris Parke, 2002.

Bodin, Jean. *Six Books of the Commonwealth*. Translated by M. J. Tooley. Oxford: Blackwell, 1955.

Bodleian Library, University of Oxford. *The Slave Trade Debate: Contemporary Writings For and Against*. Introduction by John Pinfold. Oxford: Bodleian Library, 2007.

Bok, F., with Edward Tivnan. *Escape from Slavery: The True Story of My Ten Years in Captivity—and My Journey to Freedom in America*. New York: St. Martin's Griffin, 2003.

Botterweck, G. Johannes, et al., eds. *Theological Dictionary of the Old Testament*. 14 vols. Translated by Geoffrey W. Bromiley et al. Grand Rapids: Eerdmans, 1974–2004.

Boxall, Ian. "The Many Faces of Babylon the Great: *Wirkungsgeschichte* and the Interpretation of Revelation 17." In *Studies in the Book of Revelation*, edited by Steve Moyise, 51–68. Edinburgh: T. & T. Clark, 2001.

——. *The Revelation of Saint John*. Black's New Testament Commentaries. Peabody, MA: Hendrickson, 2006.

Boxer, C. R. *The Church Militant and Iberian Expansion*. Baltimore: John Hopkins University Press, 1978.

Brennan, Denise. *What's Love Got To Do with It? Transnational Desires and Sex Tourism in the Dominican Republic*. Durham, NC: Duke University Press, 2004.

Brenner, Athalya. *The Israelite Woman: Social Role and Literary Type in Biblical Narrative*. Sheffield, UK: JSOT Press, 1994.

Brett, Mark G. *Biblical Criticism in Crisis? The Impact of the Canonical Approach on Old Testament Studies*. Cambridge: Cambridge University Press, 1991.

Briggs, John H. Y. "Baptists and the Campaign to Abolish the Slave Trade." *Baptist Quarterly* 42 (2007) 260–83.

Briggs, Sheila. "Can an Enslaved God Liberate?" *Semeia* 47 (1989) 348–57.

——. "Gender, Slavery and Technology: The Shaping of the Early Christian Moral Imagination." In *Beyond Slavery: Overcoming Its Religious and Sexual Legacies*, edited by Bernadette Brooten, 159–78. New York: Palgrave MacMillan, 2010.

——. "Paul on Bondage and Freedom in Imperial Roman Society." In *Paul and Politics: Ekklesia, Israel, Imperium, Interpretation*, edited by Richard A. Horsley, 110–24. Harrisburg, PA: Trinity, 2000.

Bristow, Edward J. *Vice and Vigilance: Purity Movements in Britain since 1700*. Dublin: Gill and Macmillan, 1977.

Broadie, Alexander, ed. *The Scottish Enlightenment: An Anthology*. Edinburgh: Canongate, 1997.

Brock, Rita Nakashima, and Susan Brooks Thistlethwaite. *Casting Stones: Prostitution and Liberation in Asia and the United States*. Minneapolis: Fortress, 1996.

Brock, Sebastian P., and Susan Ashbrook Harvey. *Holy Women of the Syrian Orient*. Berkeley: University of California Press, 1987.

Brooks-Gordon, Belinda, and Loraine Gelsthorpe. "Hiring Bodies: Male Clients and Prostitution." In *Body Lore and Laws*, edited by Andrew Bainham et al., 193–210. Oxford: Hart, 2002.

Brooten, Bernadette. "Introduction." In *Beyond Slavery: Overcoming Its Religious and Sexual Legacies*, edited by Bernadette Brooten, 1–29. New York: Palgrave MacMillan, 2010.

Brown, Christopher Leslie. *Moral Capital: Foundations of British Abolitionism*. Chapel Hill, NC: University of North Carolina Press, 2006.

Brown, Michael Joseph. "Paul's Use of ΔΟΥΛΟΣ ΧΡΙΣΤΟΥ ΙΗΣΟΥ in Romans 1:1." *JBL* 120 (2001) 723–37.

Brown, Peter. *The Body and Society: Men, Women, and Sexual Renunciation in Early Christianity*. New York: Columbia University Press. 1988.

Brueggemann, Walter. *The Book That Breathes New Life: Scriptural Authority and Biblical Authority*. Edited by Patrick D. Miller. Minneapolis: Fortress, 2005.

———. *Deuteronomy*. Nashville: Abingdon, 2001.

———. *Theology of the Old Testament: Testimony, Dispute, Advocacy*. Minneapolis: Augsburg Fortress, 1997.

———. *Truth Speaks to Power: The Countercultural Nature of Scripture*. Louisville: Westminster John Knox, 2013.

Budin, Stephanie Lynn. *The Myth of Sacred Prostitution in Antiquity*. Cambridge: Cambridge University Press, 2008.

Bullough, Vern, and Bonnie Bullough. *Prostitution: An Illustrated Social History*. New York: Crown, 1978.

Burnard, Trevor. *Mastery, Tyranny and Desire: Thomas Thistleton and His Slaves in the Anglo-Jamaican World*. Chapel Hill, NC: University of North Carolina Press, 2004.

Burnside, Jonathan P. *The Signs of Sin: Seriousness of Offence in Biblical Law*. Sheffield, UK: Sheffield Academic Press, 2003.

Burridge, Richard A. *Imitating Jesus: An Inclusive Approach to New Testament Ethics*. Grand Rapids: Eerdmans, 2007.

Bushman, Brad J., et al. "When God Sanctions Killing: Effect of Scriptural Violence on Aggression." *Psychological Science* 18 (2007) 204–7.

Byron, John. *Recent Research on Paul and Slavery*. Sheffield, UK: Phoenix, 2008.

———. *Slavery Metaphors in Early Judaism and Pauline Christianity: A Traditio-historical and Exegetical Examination*. Tübingen: Mohr Siebeck, 2003.

Cadet, Jean Robert. *Restavec: Haitian Slave Child to Middle Class American*. Austin: University of Texas Press, 1998.

Cahill, Lisa Sowle. "The New Testament and Ethics: Communities of Social Change." *Interpretation* 44 (1990) 383–95.

Califa, Pat. "Whoring in Utopia." In *The Philosophy of Sex: Contemporary Readings*, edited by A. Soble, 475–81. Lanham, MD: Rowman & Littlefield, 2002.

Callahan, Allen Dwight. *Embassy of Onesimus: The Letter of Paul to Philemon*. Valley Forge, PA: Trinity, 1997.

———. "The Letter to Philemon." In *A Postcolonial Commentary on the New Testament Writings*, edited by Fernando F. Segovia and R. S. Sugirtharajah, 329–37. London: T. & T. Clark, 2007.

———. *The Talking Book*. New Haven: Yale University Press, 2006.

Callender, Dexter E. "Servants of God(s) and Servants of Kings in Israel and the Ancient Near East." *Semeia* 83/84: *Slavery in Text and Interpretation* (1998) 67–80.

Calon, Callie. "*Adulescentes* and *Meretrices*: The Correlation between Squandered Patrimony and Prostitutes in the Parable of the Prodigal Son." *CBQ* 75 (2013) 259–78.

Camfield, Gregg. "The Moral Aesthetics of Sentimentality: A Missing Key to Uncle Tom's Cabin." *Nineteenth Century Literature* 43 (1988) 319–45.

Camp, Claudia V. *Wisdom and the Feminine in the Book of Proverbs.* Sheffield, UK: Almond, 1985.

Carey, Brycchan. *British Abolitionism and the Rhetoric of Sensibility.* London: Palgrave Macmillan, 2005.

Carmichael, Calum M. *Law and Narrative in the Bible: The Evidence of the Deuteronomic Laws and the Decalogue.* Ithaca, NY: Cornell University Press, 1985.

Carretta, Vincent, ed. *Unchained Voices: An Anthology of Black Authors in the English Speaking World of the 18th Century.* Lexington, KY: The University Press of Kentucky, 2004.

Carson, M. "The Harlot, the Beast and the Sex Trafficker: Reflections on Some Recent Feminist Interpretations of Revelation 17–18." *ExpTim* 122 (2011) 218–27.

Carter, Philippa. *The Servant-Ethic in the New Testament.* New York: Lang, 1999.

Carter, Warren. *Households and Discipleship: A Study of Matthew 19–20.* Sheffield, UK: Sheffield Academic Press, 1994.

Casey, Jay. "The Exodus Theme in the Book of Revelation against the Background of the New Testament." *Concilium* 189 (1987) 34–43.

Castelli, Elizabeth A. "Romans." In *Searching the Scriptures Volume 2: A Feminist Commentary,* edited by Elisabeth Schüssler Fiorenza, 272–300. London: SCM, 1994.

———. "Virginity and Its Meaning for Women's Sexuality in Early Christianity." *Journal of Feminist Studies in Religion* 2 (1986) 61–88.

Chapkis, W. *Live Sex Acts: Women Performing Erotic Labor.* New York: Routledge, 1997.

Chaplin, Peggy. *Maupassant: Boule de Suif.* Glasgow: University of Glasgow French and German Publications, 1988.

Childs, B. S. *Biblical Theology of the Old and New Testaments: Theological Reflection on the Christian Bible.* Minneapolis: Fortress, 1992.

Chirichigno, Gregory C. *Debt-Slavery in Israel and the Ancient Near East.* JSOT Supplement Series 141. Sheffield, UK: Sheffield Academic Press, 1993.

Chisholm Jr., Robert B. "The Christological Fulfilment of Isaiah's Servant Songs." *BSac* 163 (2006) 387–404.

Choisy, Maryse. *Psychoanalysis of the Prostitute.* New York: Philosophical Library, 1961.

Ciampa, Roy E., and Brian S. Rosner. *The First Letter to the Corinthians.* Eerdmans: Grand Rapids, 2007.

Clinton, Catherine. "Breaking the Silence: Sexual Hypocrises from Thomas Jefferson to Strom Thurmond." In *Beyond Slavery; Overcoming and Sexual Legacies,* edited by Bernadette Brooten, 213–28. New York: Palgrave Macmillan, 2010.

Cohen, Edward E. "Free and Unfree Sexual Work: An Economic Analysis of Athenian Prostitution." In *Prostitutes and Courtesans in the Ancient World,* edited by Christopher A. Faraone and Laura K. McClure, 95–124. Madison, WI: University of Wisconsin Press, 2006.

Collier, Gary D. "'That We Might Not Crave Evil': The Structure and Argument of 1 Corinthians 10:1–13." *JSNT* 55 (1994) 55–75.

Collins, John J. "The Exodus and Biblical Theology." In *Jews, Christians and the Theology of the Hebrew Scriptures,* edited by Alice Ogden Bellis and Joel S. Kamisley, 247–61. Atlanta: SBL, 2000.

Combes, I. A. H. *The Metaphor of Slavery in the Writings of the Early Church: From the New Testament to the Beginning of the Fifth Century.* JSNTSup 156. Sheffield, UK: Sheffield Academic Press, 1998.

Coontz, Stephanie. *Marriage, A History: How Love Conquered Marriage.* New York: Penguin, 2005

Corbin, Alain. *Women for Hire: Prostitution and Sexuality in France after 1850.* Cambridge, MA: Harvard University Press, 1990.

Corley, Kathleen E. *Private Women, Public Meals: Social Conflict in the Synoptic Tradition.* Peabody, MA: Hendrickson, 1993.

Cosgrove, Charles H. "A Woman's Unbound Hair in the Greco-Roman World, with Special Reference to the Story of the Sinful Woman in Luke 7:36–50." *JBL* 124 (2005) 675–92.

Countryman, L. William. *Dirt, Greed and Sex: Sexual Ethics in the New Testament and Their Implications for Today.* London: SCM, 1988.

Cowherd, Raymond G. *The Politics of English Dissent: The Religious Aspects of Liberal and Humanitarian Reform Movements from 1815 to 1848.* London: Epworth, 1956.

Coy, Maddy, ed. *Prostitution, Harm and Gender Inequality.* Farnham, UK: Ashgate, 2012.

Cranston, Maurice. *The Romantic Movement.* Oxford: Blackwell, 1994.

Craton, Michael. *Testing the Chains: Resistance to Slavery in the British West Indies.* Ithaca, NY: Cornell University Press, 1982.

Crenshaw, James L. *Joel: A New Translation with Introduction and Commentary.* The Anchor Bible. New York: Doubleday, 1995.

Croatto, J. Severino. *Exodus: A Hermeneutics of Freedom.* Maryknoll: Orbis, 1978.

Cuguano, Cuobna Ottobah. *Thoughts and Sentiments on the Evil and Wicked Traffic of the Slavery and Commerce of the Human Species.* London, 1787. Reprinted in *Unchained Voices: An Anthology of Black Authors in the English Speaking World of the 18th Century,* 150–60. Reprint. Lexington, KY: The University Press of Kentucky, 2004.

Dandamaev, Muhammad A. "Slavery (ANE)." In *The Anchor Bible Dictionary,* edited by David Noel Freedman, 58–64. New Haven: Yale University Press, 1992.

D'Angelo, Mary Rose. "Reconstructing 'Real' Women from Gospel Literature: The Case of Mary Magdalene." In *Women and Christian Origins,* edited by Ross Shepard Kraemer and Mary Rose d'Angelo, 105–49. New York: Oxford University Press, 1999.

Daube, David. *The Exodus Pattern in the Bible.* London: Faber & Faber, 1963.

Davidson, Graham "S. T. Coleridge." In *The Blackwell Companion to the Bible in English Literature,* edited by Rebecca Lemon et al., 413–24. Oxford: Blackwell, 2009.

Davidson, James. *Courtesans and Fishcakes: The Consuming Passions of Classical Athens.* London: HarperCollins, 1997.

Davies, Eryl W. *The Immoral Bible: Approaches to Biblical Ethics.* London: T. & T. Clark, 2010.

Davies, Margaret. "On Prostitution." In *The Bible and Human Society: Essays in Honour of John Rogerson,* edited by M. Daniel Carroll R. et al., 225–48. Sheffield, UK: Sheffield Academic Press, 1995.

Davis, David Brion. *The Problem of Slavery in Western Culture.* Harmondsworth, UK: Penguin, 1970.

———. *Slavery and Human Progress.* Oxford: Oxford University Press, 1984.

Dearman, John Andrew. *Property Rights in the Eighth Century Prophets.* Atlanta: Scholars, 1998.

De Beauvoir, Simone. *The Second Sex.* 1949. Reprint. London: Vintage, 1997.

De Boer, Esther. *The Mary Magdalene Cover-Up.* Translated by J. Bowden. London: T. & T. Clark, 2006.

Deconinck-Brossard, Francois. "England and France in the Eighteenth Century." In *Reading the Text: Biblical Criticism and Literary Theory*, edited by Stephen Prickett, 136–81. Oxford: Blackwell, 1991.

De Jour, Belle. *The Intimate Adventures of a London Call-Girl.* London: Weidenfeld & Nicholson, 2005.

Delacoste, Frederique, and Priscilla Alexander. *Sex Work: Writings by Women in the Sex Industry.* Pittsburgh: Cleis, 1987.

De Marneffe, Peter. *Liberalism and Prostitution.* Oxford: Oxford University Press, 2008.

De Montesquieu, Baron. *The Spirit of the Laws.* 1748. Translated and edited by Anne M. Cohler et al. Cambridge: Cambridge University Press, 1989.

deSilva, David A. *Honor, Patronage, Kinship and Purity: Unlocking New Testament Culture.* Downers Grove, IL: IVP, 2000.

De Vos, Craig S. "Once a Slave Always a Slave? Slavery, Manumission and Relational Patterns in Paul's Letter to Philemon." *JSNT* 82 (2001) 89–105.

Diamond, A. R., and Pete and Kathleen M. O'Connor. "Unfaithful Passions: Coding Women Coding Men in Jeremiah 2–3 (4:2)." *Biblical Interpretation* 4 (1996) 288–310.

Dilwyn, William, and John Lloyd. *The Case of Our Fellow-Creatures, the Oppressed Africans, Respectfully Recommended to the Serious Consideration of the Legislature of Great Britain by the People Called Quakers.* London Philip, 1783.

Dodd, Brian J. "Christ's Slave, People Pleasers and Galatians 1:10." *NTS* 42 (1996) 90–104.

Doezema, Jo. *Sex Slaves and Discourse Matters: The Construction of Trafficking.* London: Zed, 2010.

Douglas, Mary. *Purity and Danger: An Analysis of Concepts of Pollution and Taboo.* London: Routledge, 2005.

Drescher, S. *Econocide: British Slavery in the Era of Abolition.* Pittsburgh: University of Pittsburgh Press, 1977.

———. "Public Opinion and the Destruction of British Colonial Slavery." In *Slavery and British Society 1776–1846*, edited by James Walvin, 22–48. London: Macmillan, 1982.

Duff, Paul B. *Who Rides the Beast? Prophetic Rivalry and the Rhetoric of Crisis in the Churches of the Apocalypse.* Oxford: Oxford University Press, 2001.

Durham, Geoffrey. *The Spirit of the Quakers.* New Haven: Yale University Press, 2010.

Dworkin, Andrea. "Prostitution and Male Supremacy." In *Life and Death: Unapologetic Writings on the Continuing War against Women*, 139–51. London: Virago, 1997.

Eisenbaum, Pamela Michelle. *The Jewish Heroes of Christian History: Hebrews 11 in Literary Context.* Atlanta: Scholars, 1997.

Elliott, E. N., ed. *Cotton is King, and Pro-slavery Arguments.* Augusta, GA: Pritchard, Abbott and Loomis, 1860.

Elliott, John H. *A Home for the Homeless: A Sociological Exegesis of 1 Peter, Its Situation and Strategy.* London: SCM, 1982.

———. *What Is Social Scientific Criticism?* Minneapolis: Fortress, 1993.

Ellis, Markman. *The Politics of Sensibility: Race, Gender and Commerce in the Sentimental Novel.* Cambridge: Cambridge University Press, 1996.

Engberg-Pedersen, Troels. *Cosmology and the Self in the Apostle Paul: The Material Spirit.* Oxford: Oxford University Press, 2010.

Engels, Friedrich. *The Origin of the Family, Private Property and the State.* Reprint. London: Penguin, 1985.

Engerman, Stanley, Seymour Drescher, and Robert Paquette, eds. *Slavery: Oxford Readers.* Oxford: Oxford University Press, 2001.

Equiano, Oloudah. *The Interesting Narrative and Other Writings.* 1789. Reprint. London: Penguin, 2003.

Ericsson, Lars O. "Charges against Prostitution: An Attempt at a Philosophical Assessment." *Ethics* 90 (1980) 335–66.

Eslinger, Lyle. "Freedom or Knowledge? Perspective and Purpose in the Exodus Narrative. (Exodus 1–15)." *JSOT* 16 (1991) 43–60.

Fabre, Cécile. *Whose Body Is It Anyway? Justice and the Integrity of the Person.* Oxford: Oxford University Press, 2006.

Farley, Melissa, ed. *Prostitution, Trafficking, and Traumatic Stress.* Binghamton, NY: Haworth, 2004.

Finley, Moses I., ed. *Classical Slavery.* London: Cass, 1987.

Fiorenza, Elizabeth Schüssler. *The Book of Revelation: Justice and Judgement.* 2nd ed. Minneapolis: Augsburg Fortress, 1988.

———. *In Memory of Her: A Feminist Theological Reconstruction of Christian Origins.* London: SCM, 1983.

———. *The Power of the Word: Scripture and the Rhetoric of Empire.* Minneapolis: Fortress, 2007.

———. "The Praxis of Co-Equal Discipleship." In *Paul and Empire: Religion and Power in Roman Imperial Society,* edited by Richard A. Horsley, 224–41. Harrisburg, PA: Trinity, 1997.

———. "Redemption as Liberation: Apoc 1:5f and 5:9 f." *CBQ* 36 (1974) 220–32.

———. *Rhetoric and Ethic: The Politics of Biblical Studies.* Minneapolis : Fortress, 1999.

Fisch, Audrey A. *American Slaves in Victorian England: Abolitionist Politics in Popular Religion and Culture.* Cambridge: Cambridge University Press, 2000.

Fishbane, Michael. *Biblical Interpretation in Ancient Israel.* Oxford: Clarendon, 1985.

Fisher, Philip. *Hard Facts: Setting and Form in the American Novel.* New York: Oxford University Press, 1985.

Fisher, Trevor. *Prostitution and the Victorians.* Stroud, UK: Sutton, 1997.

Fogel, Robert William. *Without Consent or Contract: The Rise and Fall of American Slavery.* New York: Norton, 1989.

Forsyth, Sarah. *Slave Girl.* London: Blake, 2010.

Fowl, Stephen E. *Engaging Scripture: A Model for Theological Interpretation.* Oxford: Blackwell, 1998.

Fox-Genovese, Elizabeth, and Eugene D. Genovese. *The Mind of the Master Class: History and Faith in the Southern Slaveholders' Worldview.* New York: Cambridge University Press, 2005.

Fretheim, Terence E. "Law in the Service of Life: Dynamic Understanding of Law in Deuteronomy." In *A God So Near: Essays in Old Testament Theology in Honor of Patrick D. Miller,* edited by Brent A. Strawn and Nancy R. Bowen, 183–200. Winona Lake, IN: Eisenbrauns, 2003.

Frisby, David, and Mike Featherstone, eds. *Simmel on Culture.* London: Sage, 1997.

Frost, J. William. *The Quaker Origins of Antislavery.* Norwood, PA: Norwood Editions, 1980.

Frymer-Kensky, Tikva. *In the Wake of the Goddesses: Women, Culture and the Biblical Transformation of Pagan Myth.* New York: Fawcett Columbine, 1992.

———. "Pollution, Purification and Purgation in Biblical Israel." In *The Word of the Lord Shall Go Forth: Essays in Honour of David Noel Freedman in Celebration of his Sixtieth Birthday*, edited by Carol L. Meyers and M. O'Connor, 339–414. Winona Lake, IN: Eisenbrauns, 1983.

———. "Virginity in the Bible." In *Gender and Law in the Hebrew Bible and the Ancient Near East*, edited by V. H. Matthews et al., 79–96. Sheffield, UK: Sheffield Academic Press, 1998.

Furst, Lilian R., and Peter N. Skrine. *Naturalism*. London: Methuen, 1971.

Gangoli, Geetanjali. "Prostitution in India: Laws, Debates and Responses." In *International Approaches to Prostitution: Law and Policy in Europe and Asia*, edited by Nicole Westmarland and Geetanjali Gongoli, 115–39. Bristol, UK: Policy, 2006.

Garland, David E. *1 Corinthians*. Grand Rapids: Baker Academic, 2003.

Garnsey, Peter. *Ideas of Slavery from Aristotle to Augustine*. Cambridge: Cambridge University Press, 1996.

Genovese, Eugene D. *Roll Jordan Roll: The World the Slaves Made*. New York: Pantheon, 1974.

Gignilliat, Mark. *Paul and Isaiah's Servants: Paul's Theological Reading of Isaiah 40–66 in 2 Corinthians 5:14—6:10*. London: T. & T. Clark, 2007.

Giobbe, Evelina. "Confronting the Liberal Lies about Prostitution." In *The Sexual Liberals and the Attack on Feminism*, edited by Dorchen Leidholdt and Janice G. Raymond, 67–81. New York: Pergamon, 1990.

Glancy, Jennifer A. "House Reading and Field Readings: The Discourse of Slavery and Biblical/Cultural Studies." In *Biblical Studies, Cultural Studies: The Third Sheffield Colloquium*, edited by J. Cheryl Exum and Stephen D. Moore, 460–77. Sheffield, UK: Sheffield Academic Press, 1998.

———. "Obstacles to Slaves' Participation in the Corinthian Church." *JBL* 117 (1998) 481–501.

———. *Slavery in Early Christianity*. New York: Oxford University Press, 2002.

Glancy, Jennifer A., and Stephen D. Moore. "How Typical a Roman Prostitute Is Revelation's 'Great Whore'?" *JBL* 130 (2011) 551–69.

Goldingay, John. *Approaches to Old Testament Interpretation*. Leicester, UK: IVP, 1981.

———. *Models for Scripture*. Grand Rapids: Eerdmans, 1994.

———. *Old Testament Theology Vol. 3 Israel's Life*. Downers Grove, IL: IVP Academic, 2009.

Gombis, Timothy G. *A Radical New Humanity: The Function of the Haustafel in Ephesians*. *JETS* 48 (2005) 317–30.

Goodfriend, Elaine Adler. "Could *keleb* in Deuteronomy 23:19 Actually Refer to a Canine?" In *Pomegranates and Golden Bells: Studies in Biblical, Jewish, and Near Eastern Ritual, Law, and Literature in Honor of Jacob Milgrom*, edited by David P. Wright et al., 381–97. Winona Lake, IN: Eisenbrauns, 1995.

Gordon, Robert P. *Hebrews*. 2nd ed. Sheffield, UK: Sheffield Pheonix Press, 2008.

Guider, Margaret Eletta. *Daughters of Rahab: Prostitution and the Church of Liberation in Brazil*. Boston: Harvard Theological Studies 1995.

Gupta, Rahila. *Enslaved: The New British Slavery*. London: Portobello, 2007.

Haas, G. H. "Slave, Slavery." In *Dictionary of the Old Testament: Pentateuch*, edited by David W. Baker & T. Desmond Alexander, 778–83. Downers Grove, IL: IVP, 2003.

Halbertal, Moshel, and Avishai Margalit. *Idolatry*. Translated by Naomi Goldblum. Cambridge: Harvard University Press, 1992.

Harding, Vincent. "Religion and Resistance among Antebellum Slaves 1800–1860." In *African-American Religion: Interpretive Essays in History and Culture,* edited by Timothy E. Fulop and Albert J. Raboteau, 107–29. London: Routledge, 1997.

Harper, Kyle. "Porneia: The Making of a Christian Sexual Norm." *JBL* 131 (2011) 363–83.

Harrelson Walter J. *Hebrew Bible: History of Interpretation.* Nashville: Abingdon, 2004.

Harrill, J. Albert. *The Manumission of Slaves in Early Christianity.* Tübingen: Mohr (Siebeck), 1995.

———. "Slavery." In *The New Interpreter's Dictionary of the Bible,* edited by Katherine Doob Sakenfield et al., 299–308. Nashville: Abingdon, 2009.

———. "The Use of the New Testament in the American Slave Controversy: A Case History in the Hermeneutical Tension between Biblical Criticism and Christian Moral Debate." *Religion and American Culture* 10 (2000) 149–86.

———. "The Vice of Slave Dealers in Greco-Roman Society: The Use of a Topos in 1 Timothy 1:10." *JBL* 118 (1999) 97–122.

Harris, Murray J. *Slave of Christ: A New Testament Metaphor for Total Devotion to Christ.* Downers Grove, IL: IVP, 1999.

Harris, Raymond. "Scriptural Researches on the Licitness of the Slave Trade, Shewing its Conformity with the Principles of Natural and Revealed Religion, Delineated in the Sacred Writings of the Word of God." 1788. Reprinted in Bodleian Library, *The Slave Trade Debate: Contemporary Writings For and Against,* 174–245. Oxford: Bodlean Library, 2007.

Harris, Victor. "Allegory to Analogy in the Interpretation of Scriptures." *Philological Quarterly* 45 (1966) 1–23.

Hartley, John E. *Leviticus 1–27.* Word Biblical Commentaries. Waco, TX: Word, 1992.

Haskins, Susan. *Mary Magdalene: Myth and Metaphor.* London: Harper Collins, 1993.

Hauerwas, Stanley. *The Peaceable Kingdom: A Primer in Christian Ethics.* Notre Dame, IN: University of Notre Dame Press, 1983.

Hayes, Diana. "Reflections on Slavery." In *Change in Official Catholic Moral Teachings,* edited by Charles E. Curran, 65–75. Mahwah, NJ: Paulist, 2003.

Haykin, Michael A. G., and Kenneth J. Stewart. *The Emergence of Evangelicalism: Exploring Historical Continuities.* Nottingham, UK: Apollos, 2008.

Hays, Richard B. *The Moral Vision of the New Testament: A Contemporary Introduction of New Testament Ethics.* London: T. & T. Clark, 1996.

Heasman, Kathleen. *Evangelicals in Action: An Appraisal of Their Social Work in the Victorian Era.* London: Bles, 1962.

Hess, Richard S. *Joshua: An Introduction and Commentary.* Leicester, UK: IVP, 1996.

Hill, Christopher. *The World Turned Upside Down: Radical Ideas During the English Revolution.* London: Penguin, 1972.

Hilton, Boyd. *The Age of Atonement: The Influence of Evangelicalism on Social and Economic Thought 1785–1863.* Oxford: Clarendon, 1968.

Hobson, Barbara Meil. *Uneasy Virtue: The Politics of Prostitution and the American Reform Tradition.* New York: Basic, 1987.

Hochschild, A. *Bury the Chains: The British Struggle to Abolish Slavery.* London: Macmillan, 2005.

Hodge, Charles. *Systematic Theology,* Vol. 1. Peabody, MA: Hendrickson, 2003.

———. *View of the Subject of Slavery Contained in* The Biblical Repertory *for April, 1836 in which the Scriptural Argument, It Is Believed, Is Very Clearly and Justly Exhibited.* Pittsburgh, 1836.

Home Office. *Paying the Price: A Consultation Paper on Prostitution*. London: Home Office Communication Directorate, July 2004.

Hopkins, John Henry. *A Scriptural, Ecclesiastical, and Historical View of Slavery from the Days of the Patriarch Abraham to the Nineteenth Century*. New York: Pooley, 1864.

Hopkins, Samuel. *A Dialogue, concerning the Slavery of the Africans; Shewing It to Be the Duty and Interest of the American Colonies to Emancipate All Their African Slaves: With an Address to the Owners of Such Slaves*. Norwich, CT: Spooner, 1776.

Hoppe. Leslie J. *There Shall Be No Poor Among You: Poverty in the Bible*. Nashville: Abingdon, 2004.

Hornsby, Theresa, J. "'Israel Has Become a Worthless Thing': Re-reading Gomer in Hosea 1–3." *JSOT* 82 (1999) 115–28.

———. "The Woman Is a Sinner/The Sinner Is a Woman." In *A Feminist Companion to Luke*, edited by Amy-Jill Levine, 121–32. Sheffield, UK: Sheffield Academic Press, 2002.

Horsley, Richard A. "The Slave Systems of Classical Antiquity and Their Reluctant Recognition by Modern Scholars." *Semeia* 83/84. *Slavery in Text and Interpretation* (1998) 19–66.

Houston, Walter. *Purity and Monotheism: Clean and Unclean Animals in Biblical Law*. Sheffield, UK: Sheffield Academic Press, 1993.

Howse, Ernest Marshall. *Saints in Politics: The "Clapham Sect" and the Growth of Freedom*. London: Allen & Unwin, 1952.

Hubbard Jr., Robert L. "The Divine Redeemer: Toward a Biblical Theology of Redemption." In *Reading the Hebrew Bible for a New Millenium, Vol. 1: Form, Content, and Theological Perspective*, edited by Wonil Kim et al., 188–204. Harrisburg, PA: Trinity, 2000.

Huber, Lynn R. *Like a Bride Adorned: Reading Metaphor in John's Apocalypse*. London: T. & T. Clark, 2007.

Hugenberger, G. P. "The Servant of the Lord in the 'Servant Songs' of Isaiah: A Second Moses Figure." In *The Lord's Annointed: Interpretation of Old Testament Messianic Texts*, edited by Philip E. Satterthwaite, Richard S. Hess, and Gordon J. Wenham, 105–40. Carlisle, UK: Paternoster, 1995.

Hultgren, Arland J. *The Parables of Jesus: A Commentary*. Grand Rapids: Eerdmans, 2000.

Hutchison, John C. "Women, Gentiles, and the Messianic Mission in Matthew's Genealogy." *BSac* 158 (2001) 152–64.

Ilan, Tal. *Jewish Women in Greco-Roman Palestine: An Inquiry into Image and Status*. Tübingen: Mohr, 1995.

Ipsen, Avaren. *Sex Working in the Bible*. London: Equinox, 2009.

Ivison, Irene. *Fiona's Story: A Tragedy of our Times*. London: Virago, 1997.

Jackson, Bernard S. "Biblical Laws of Slavery: A Comparative Approach." In *Slavery and Other Forms of Unfree Labour*, edited by Léonie Archer, 86–101. London: Routledge, 1988.

———. *Wisdom Laws: A Study of the Mishpatim of Exodus 21:1—22:16*. Oxford: Oxford University Press, 2006.

Jantzen, Waldemar. *Old Testament Ethics: A Paradigmatic Approach*. Louisville, KY: Westminster John Knox, 1994.

Janzen, J. Gerald. *Exodus*. Louisville, KY: Westminster John Knox, 1997.

Jasper, David. *The Sacred and Secular Canon in Romanticism*. Basingstoke, UK: Macmillan, 1999.

Jensen, Joseph. "Does *Porneia* Mean Fornication? A Critique of Bruce J. Malina." *NovT* 20 (1978) 161–84.

Jeremias, Joachim. *Jerusalem in the Time of Jesus: An Investigation into Economic and Social Conditions during the New Testament Period*. Philadelphia: Fortress, 1969.

Johnson, B. Julie. "Ain't I a Human?" *Prism* 2010, 35–38, 47.

Johnson, Sylvester A. "The Bible, Slavery and the Problem of Authority." In *Beyond Slavery: Overcoming Its Religious and Sexual Legacies*, edited by Bernadette Brooten, 231–48. New York: Palgrave Macmillan 2010.

Jordan, Jane. *Josephine Butler*. London: Continuum, 2001.

Kahl, Werner. "Growing Together: Challenges and Chances in the Encounter of Critical and Intuitive Interpreters of the Bible." In *Reading Otherwise: Socially Engaged Biblical Scholars Reading with their Local Communities*, edited by Gerald O. West, 147–58. Atlanta: SBL, 2007.

Kaiser, Otto. *Isaiah 13–39: A Commentary*. London SCM, 1974.

Kaiser, Walter C. *Toward Old Testament Ethics*. Grand Rapids: Zondervan, 1983.

Kant, Immanuel. *Anthropology from a Pragmatic Point of View*. Edited and translated by Robert B. Louden. Cambridge: Cambridge University Press, 2006.

———. *Lectures on Ethics*. Translated by L. Infield. London: Methuen, 1979.

Kara, Siddharth. *Sex Trafficking: Inside the Business of Modern Slavery*. New York: Columbia University Press, 2009.

Karras, Ruth Mazo. *Common Women: Prostitution and Sexuality in Medieval England*. New York: Oxford University Press, 1996.

Keesmaat, Sylia C. *Paul and His Story: (Re)Interpreting the Exodus Tradition*. Sheffield, UK: Sheffield Academic Press, 1999.

Kempadoo, Kamala, and Jo Doezema, eds. *Global Sex Workers: Rights, Resistance, and Redefinition*. New York: Routledge, 1998.

Kenrick, Francis Patrick. *The Acts of the Apostles, the Epistles of Saint Paul, the Catholic Epistles and the Apocalypse*. New York, 1981.

Kidd, Colin. *The Forging of Races: Race and Scripture in the Protestant Atlantic World, 1600–2000*. Cambridge: Cambridge University Press, 2006.

Kidd, Reggie M. *Wealth and Beneficence in the Pastoral Epistles: A "Bourgeois" Form of Early Christianity?* Atlanta: Scholars, 1990.

Kidd, Thomas S. *The Great Awakening: The Roots of Evangelical Christianity in Colonial America*. New Haven: Yale, 2007.

Kim, Jean M. "Uncovering Her Wickedness: An Inter(con)textual Reading of Revelation 17 from a Postcolonial Feminist Perspective." *JSNT* 73 (1999) 61–81.

King, Gilbert. *Woman, Child for Sale: The New Slave Trade in the 21st Century*. New York: Chamberlain, 2004.

Kirchhoff, Renate. *Die Sünde gegen den eigenten Leib: studien zu Πόρνη und Πορνεία in 1 Kor 6:12–20 und dem sozio-kulturellen Kontext der paulisichen Adressaten*. Göttingen: Vandenhoek & Ruprecht, 1994.

Kirk-Duggan, Cheryl A. "Let My People Go! Threads of Exodus in African-American Narratives." In *Voices from the Margin: Interpreting the Bible in the Third World*, edited by R. S. Sugirtharajah, 258–78. Maryknoll, NY: Orbis, 2006.

Klawans, J. *Impurity and Sin in Ancient Judaism*. New York: Oxford University Press, 2000.

Klein, Lilian R. *The Triumph of Irony in the Book of Judges*. Sheffield, UK: Almond, 1988.

Kling, David W. *The Bible in History: How the Texts Have Shaped the Times*. Oxford: Oxford University Press, 2004.

Knight, George W. III, *The Pastoral Epistles: A Commentary on the Greek Text*. New International Greek Testament Commentary. Grand Rapids: Eerdmans, 1992.

Knowles, Michael P. "'Everyone Who Hears These Words of Mine': Parables on Discipleship (Matt 7:24–27//Luke 6:47–49; Luke 14:28–33; Luke 17:7–10; Matt 20:1–16)." In *The Challenge of Jesus' Parables*, edited by Richard N. Longenecker, 286–305. Grand Rapids: Eerdmans, 2000.

Koester, Craig R. "Roman Slave Trade and the Critique of Babylon in Revelation 18." *CBQ* 70 (2008) 766–86.

Kolchin, Peter. *American Slavery 1619–1877*. London: Penguin, 1993.

Koltun-Fromm, Naomi. *Hermeneutics of Holiness: Ancient Jewish and Christian Notions of Sexuality and Religious Community*. New York: Oxford University Press, 2010.

Kovacs, Judith, and Christopher Rowland. *Revelation*. Oxford: Blackwell, 2004.

Kriger, Diane. *Sex Rewarded, Sex Punished: A Study of the Status "Female Slave" in Early Jewish Law*. Boston: Academic Studies, 2011.

Kuan, Kah-Jin, and Mai-Anh Le Tran. "Reading Race Reading Rehab: A 'Broad' Asian American Reading of a 'Broad' Other." In *Postcolonial Interventions: Essays in Honour of R. S. Sugirtharajah*, edited by Tat-Siong Benny Liew, 27–44. Sheffield, UK: Pheonix, 2009.

Lampe, Peter. "The Language of Equality in Early Christian House Churches: A Constructivist Approach." In *Early Christian Families in Context: An Interdisciplinary Dialogue*, edited by David L. Balch and Carolyn Osiek, 73–83. Grand Rapids: Eerdmans, 2003.

Lapide, Pinchas. "Exodus in the Jewish Tradition." In *Exodus: A Lasting Paradigm*, edited by Bastiann M. F. van Iersel, 47–55. Edinburgh: T. & T. Clark, 1987.

Ledbetter, T. Mark. "Changing Sensibilities: The Puritan Mind and the Romantic Revolution in Early American Religious Thought." In *The Interpretation of Belief: Coleridge, Schleiermacher and Romanticism*, edited by David Jasper, 176–84. Basingstoke, UK: Macmillan, 1986.

Lee, Catherine. *Policing Prostitution 1856–1886*. London: Pickering & Chatto, 2013.

Lee, Debbie. *Slavery and the Romantic Imagination*. Philadelphia: University of Pennsylvania Press, 2002.

Lee, Maurice S. *Slavery, Philosophy, and American Literature*. Cambridge: Cambridge University Press, 2005.

Lemos, T. M. *Marriage Gifts and Social Change in Ancient Palestine 1200BCE to 200CE*. Cambridge: Cambridge University Press, 2010.

Lerner, Gerda. *The Creation of Patriarchy*. New York: Oxford University Press, 1986.

Lerum, Kari. "Twelve Step Feminism Makes Sex Workers Sick." In *Sex Work and Sex Workers*, edited by Barry M. Dank and Roberto Refinetti, 7–36. New Brunswick: Transaction, 1999.

Lester, Julius. *To Be a Slave*. New York: Puffin, 1968.

Leuchter, Mark. "The Manumission Laws in Leviticus and Deuteronomy: The Jeremiah Connection." *JBL* 127 (2008) 635–53.

Levenson, Jon D. *The Hebrew Bible, the Old Testament and Historical Criticism*. Louisville, KY: Westminster John Knox, 1993.

Levine, Amy-Jill. "Rahab in the New Testament." In *Women in Scripture: A Dictionary of Named and Unnamed Women in the Hebrew Bible, the Apocryphal /Deuterocanonical Books, and the New Testament*, edited by Carol Meyers, Toni Craven, and Ross S. Kraemer, 141–42. Boston: Houghton Mifflin, 2000.

Lewis, Ann, and Markman Ellis, eds. *Prostitution and Eighteenth Century Culture: Sex, Commerce and Morality*. London: Pickering & Chatto, 2012.

Lewis, Lloyd A. "An African American Appraisal of the Philemon-Paul-Onesimus Triangle." In *Stony the Road We Trod: African American Biblical Interpretation*, edited by Cain Hope Felder, 232–45. Minneapolis: Fortress, 1991.

Lienhard, Joseph T. *The Bible, the Church, and Authority: The Canon of the Christian Bible in History and Theology*. Collegeville, MN: Glazier, 1995.

Lierman, John. *The New Testament Moses: Christian Perceptions of Moses and Israel in the Setting of Jewish Religion*. Tübingen: Mohr Siebeck, 2004.

Logan, Deborah Anne. *Fallenness In Victorian Women's Writing: Marry, Stitch, Die or do Worse*. Columbia: University of Missouri Press, 1998.

Lohse, Eduard. *Colossians and Philemon*. Minneapolis: Fortress, 1971.

Luddy, Maria. *Prostitution and Irish Society*. Cambridge: Cambridge University Press, 2007.

Lyall, Francis. *Slaves, Citizens, Sons: Legal Metaphors in the Epistles*. Grand Rapids: Zondervan, 1984.

MacDonald, Margaret Y. *The Pauline Churches: A Socio-Historical Study of Institutionalization in the Pauline and Deutero-Pauline Writings*. Cambridge: Cambridge University Press, 1988.

———. "Slavery, Sexuality and the House Churches: A Reassessment of Colossians 3:18—4:1 in Light of New Research on the Roman Family." *NTS* 53 (2007) 94–113.

MacKinnon, Catherine. *Feminism Unmodified: Discourses on Life and Law*. Cambridge: Cambridge University Press, 1987.

Magdelene F. Rachel. "Ancient NE Treaty-Curses and the Ultimate Texts of Terror: A Study of the Language of Divine Sexual Abuse in the Prophetic Corpus." In *Feminist Companion to the Latter Prophets*, edited by Athalya Brenner, 326–52. Sheffield, UK: Sheffield Academic Press, 1995.

Maher, JaneMaree, et al. *Sex Work: Labour, Mobility and Sexual Services*. Abingdon, UK: Routledge, 2013.

Mahood, Linda. *The Magdalenes: Prostitution in the Nineteenth Century*. London: Routledge, 1990.

Malarek, Victor. *The Natashas: The New Global Sex Trade*. London: Vision, 2004.

Marchal, Joseph A. "The Usefulness of an Onesimus: The Sexual Use of Slaves and Paul's Letter to Philemon." *JBL* 130 (2011) 740–99.

Marshall, I Howard. *A Critical and Exegetical Commentary on the Pastoral Epistles*. International Critical Commentaries. Edinburgh: T. & T. Clark, 1999.

Marshall, Jay W. *Israel and the Book of the Covenant: An Anthropological Approach to Biblical Law*. Atlanta: Scholars, 1993.

Martin, Clarice J. "The Haustafeln (Household Codes) in African American Biblical Interpretation: Free Slaves and Subordinate Women." In *Stony the Road We Trod: African American Biblical Interpretation*, edited by Cain Hope Felder, 206–31. Minneapolis: Fortress, 1991.

Martin, Dale B. *The Corinthian Body*. New Haven: Yale University Press, 1995.

———. *Slavery as Salvation: The Metaphor of Slavery in Pauline Christianity*. New Haven: Yale University Press, 1990.

Martineau, Harriet. *Society in America*. New York: Unders & Otley, 1837.

Marx, Karl, and Frederick Engels. *Economic and Philosophic Manuscripts of 1844*. Translated by M. Milligan. Moscow: Progress, 1964.

Mather, Coton. *The Negro Christianised: An Essay to Excite and Assist the Good Work, the Instruction of Negro-Servants in Christianity*. Boston: Green, 1706.

Matthews, Victor H. "The Anthropology of Slavery in the Covenant Code." In *Theory and Method in Biblical and Cuneiform Law: Revision, Interpolation and Development*, edited by Bernard M. Levinson, 119–35. Sheffield, UK: Sheffield Academic Press, 1994.

Matthews, Victor H., and Don C. Benjamin. *Social World of Ancient Israel 1250–587BCE*. Peabody, MA: Hendrickson, 1993.

Matthews, Victor H. "The Anthropology of Slavery in the Covenant Code." In *Theory and Method in Biblical and Cuneiform Law: Revision, Interpolation and Development*, edited by Bernard M. Levinson, 119–35. Sheffield, UK: Sheffield Academic Press, 1994.

Matthews, Victor H., and Don C. Benjamin. *Social World of Ancient Israel 1250–587 BCE*. Peabody, MA: Hendrickson, 1993.

Maupassant, Guy de. *Butterball*. Translated by Andrew Brown. London: Hesperus, 2003.

Maxwell, J. F. *Slavery and the Catholic Church: The History of Catholic Teaching Concerning the Moral Legitimacy of the Institution of Slavery*. London: Rose, 1975.

May, Alistair Scott. *"The Body for the Lord": Sex and Identity in 1 Corinthians 5–7*. London: T. & T. Clark, 2004.

Mayhew, Henry, and Bracebridge Hemyng. *London Labour and the London Poor: A Cyclopedia of the Condition and Earning of Those That Will Work, Those That Cannot Work, and Those That Will Not Work!* Vol. 4. London: Griffin, Bohn. & Co., 1862.

Mbuwayesango, Dora Rudo. "Canaanite Women and Israelite Women in Deuteronomy: The Intersection of Sexism and Imperialism." In *Postcolonial Interventions: Essays in Honour of R. S. Sugirtharajah*, edited by Tat-Siong Benny Liew, 45–57. Sheffield, UK: Pheonix, 2009.

McCann, Edwin. "John Locke." In *A Companion to Early Modern Philosophy*, edited by Steven Nadler, 354–74. Oxford: Blackwell, 2008.

McDonald, James I. H. *Biblical Interpretation and Christian Ethics*. Cambridge: Cambridge University Press 1993.

McDonald, L. M. *The Biblical Canon: Its Origin, Transmission and Authority*. Peabody, MA: Hendrickson, 2007.

McEleney, Neil J. "The Vice Lists of the Pastoral Epistles." *CBQ* 36 (1974) 203–19.

McGinn, Thomas A. J. *The Economy of Prostitution in the Roman World: A Study of Social History & the Brothel*. Ann Arbor, MI: University of Michigan Press, 2004.

———. *Prostitution, Sexuality and the Law in Ancient Rome*. New York: Oxford University Press, 1998.

———. "Zoning Shame in the Roman City." In *Prostitutes and Courtesans in the Ancient World*, edited by Christopher A. Faraone and Laura K. McClure, 161–76. Madison, WI: University of Wisconsin Press, 2006.

McGreevy, John T. *Catholicism and American Freedom*. New York: Norton, 2003.

McHugh, Paul. *Prostitution and Victorian Social Reform*. London: Croom Helm, 1980.

McKane, William. *Proverbs: A New Approach*. London: SCM, 1970.

Meeks, Wayne A. "'And Rose Up to Play': Midrash and Paraenesis in 1 Corinthians 10:1–22." *JSNT* 16 (1982) 64–78.

———. *The First Urban Christians: The Social World of the Apostle Paul*. New Haven: Yale University Press, 1983.

———. "The 'Haustafeln' and American Slavery: A Hermeneutical Challenge." In *Theology and Ethics in Paul and His Interpreters*, edited by. E. Lovering and J. Sumney, 232–53. Nashville, TN: Abingdon, 1996.

———. *The Origins of Christian Morality: The First Two Centuries.* New Haven: Yale University Press, 1993.

Mein, Andrew. "Ezekiel's Women in Christian Interpretation: The Case of Ezekiel 16." In *After Ezekiel: Essays on the Reception of a Difficult Prophet*, edited by Paul M. Joyce & Andrew Mein, 159–83. London: T. & T. Clark, 2011.

Menn, Esther Marie. *Judah and Tamar (Gen 38) in Ancient Jewish Exegesis: Studies in Literary Form and Exegesis.* Leiden: Brill, 1997.

Meyers, Carole. *Rediscovering Eve: Ancient Israelite Women in Context.* Oxford: Oxford University Press, 2013.

Miles, Glen, and Christa Foster Crawford. *Stopping the Traffick: A Christian Response to Sexual Exploitation and Trafficking.* Eugene, OR: Wipf & Stock, 2014.

Mill, J. S. *The Subjection of Women.* 1869. Reprint. Cambridge: MIT Press, 1970.

Miller, James E. "A Critical Response to Karen Adams's Reinterpretation of Hosea 4:13–14." *JBL* 128 (2009) 503–6.

Miller, Susan. *Women in Mark's Gospel.* London: T. & T. Clark, 2004.

Milgrom, Jacob. *Leviticus 17–22: A New Translation with Introduction and Commentary.* New York: Doubleday, 2000.

Minkema, Kennet P., and Harry S. Stout. "The Edwardsean Tradition and the Antislavery Debate." *Journal of American History* 92 (2005) 47–74.

Montegu, Barbara. *The Histories of Some of the Penitents of the Magdalen-House.* Edited by Jennie Batchelor and Megan Hiatt. London: Pickering & Chatto, 2007.

Monto, Martin A. "Why Men Seek out Prostitutes." In *Sex for Sale: Prostitution, Pornography and the Sex Industry*, edited by Ronald Weitzer, 67–83. London: Routledge, 2000.

Moore, Rosemary. *The Light in Their Consciences: Early Quakers in Britain 1646–66.* University Park, PA: The Pennsylvania State University Press, 2000.

Morgan, Kenneth. *Slavery in America: A Reader and Guide.* Edinburgh: Edinburgh University Press, 2005.

Mott, Stephen Charles. *Biblical Ethics and Social Change.* Rev. ed. Oxford: Oxford University Press, 2011.

Murphy, Roland E. "Wisdom and Eros in Proverbs 1–9." *CBQ* 50 (1988) 60–63.

Naphy, William. *Sex Crimes: From Renaissance to Enlightenment.* Stroud, UK: Tempus, 2002.

Nasuti, Henry P. "Identity, Identification and Imitation: The Narrative Hermeneutics of Biblical Law." *Journal of Law and Religion* 4 (1986) 9–23.

Nazer, Mende, and Damien Lewis. *Slave.* London: Virago, 2007.

Neville, Richard W. "A Reassessment of the Radical Nature of Job's Ethic in Job 31:13–15." *VT* 53 (2003) 181–200.

Nicholson, Ernest. "Deuteronomy's Vision of Israel." In *Storia et Tradizione de Israele: Scritti in Onore di J. Alberto Soggin*, edited by D. Garrone and F. Israel, 191–203. Brescia, Italy: Paideia, 1991.

Niditch, Susan. "The Wronged Woman Righted: An Analysis of Genesis 38." *HTR* 72 (1979) 143–49.

Noble, Paul R. *The Canonical Approach: A Critical Reconstruction of the Hermeneutics of Brevard S. Childs.* Leiden: Brill, 1995.

Nogueira, Paulo. "Exodus in Latin America." In *The Oxford Handbook of the Reception History of the Bible*, edited by Michael Lieb et al., 447–59. Oxford: Oxford University Press, 2011.

Noll, Mark A. *America's God: From Jonathan Edwards to Abraham Lincoln*. Oxford: Oxford University Press, 2002.

———. *The Civil War as a Theological Crisis*. Chapel Hill, NC: University of North Carolina Press, 2006.

———. "The Image of the United States as a Biblical Nation, 1776–1865." In *The Bible in America: Essays in Cultural History*, edited by Nathan O. Hatch and Mark A. Noll, 39–58. New York: Oxford University Press, 1982.

———. *The Princeton Theology 1812–1921: Scripture, Science and Theological Method from Archibald Alexander to Benjamin Breckenridge Warfield*. Grand Rapids: Baker, 1983.

Nordling, John G. "Onesimus Fugitivus: A Defense of the Runaway Slave Hypothesis in Philemon." *JSNT* 41 (1991) 97–119.

O'Brien, Julia M. *Challenging Prophetic Metaphor: Theology and Ideology in the Prophets*. Louisville, KY: Westminster John Knox, 2008.

O'Connor, Monica, and Grainne Healey. *The Links between Prostitution and Sex Trafficking: A Briefing Handbook*. Brussels: European Women's Lobby, 2006.

Ogletree, Thomas W. *The Use of the Bible in Christian Ethics*. Oxford: Blackwell, 1984.

O'Neill, Maggie. *Prostitution and Feminism: Towards a Politics of Feeling*. Cambridge: Polity, 2001.

Ortlund, Raymond C. Jr. *Whoredom: God's Unfaithful Wife in Biblical Theology*. Leicester, UK: Apollos, 1996.

Oshatz, Molly. *Slavery and Sin: The Fight against Slavery and the Rise of Liberal Protestantism*. Oxford: Oxford University Press, 2012.

Osiek, Carolyn. "Slaves, Porneia, and the Limits of Obedience." In *Early Christian Families in Context: An Interdisciplinary Dialogue*, edited by David L. Balch and Carolyn Osiek, 255–74. Grand Rapids: Eerdmans, 2003.

Osiek, Carolyn, and David L. Balch. *Families in the New Testament World: Households and House Churches*. Louisville, KY: Westminster John Knox, 1997.

Otis, Leah Lydia. *Prostitution in Medieval Society: The History of an Urban Institution in Languedoc*. Chicago: University of Chicago Press, 1985.

Paige, Terence. "Stoicism, ἐλευθερία and Community at Corinth." In *Christianity at Corinth: The Quest for the Pauline Church*, edited by Edward Adams and David G. Horrell, 207–18. Louisville, KY: Westminster John Knox, 2004.

Palmer, T. Vail. "Did William Penn Diverge Significantly from George Fox in his Understanding of the Quaker Message?" *Quaker Studies* 11 (2006) 59–70.

Parent-Duchâtelet, A. J. B. *De la Prostitution dans la Ville de Paris, Considérée sous le Rapport de l'Hygiène Publique, de la Morale, et de l'Administration*. Paris: Bailllere et fils, 1857.

Patte, Daniel. *Ethics of Biblical Interpretation: A Re-evaluation*. Louisville, KY: Westminster John Knox, 1995.

Patterson, Orlando. *Slavery and Social Death: A Comparative Study*. Cambridge: Harvard University Press, 1982.

Paul, Ian "The Book of Revelation: Image, Symbol and Metaphor." In *Studies in the Book of Revelation*, edited by Steve Moyise, 131–47. Edinburgh: T. & T. Clark, 2001.

Pelikan, Jaroslav. *Mary through the Centuries: Her Place in the History of Culture*. New Haven: Yale University Press, 1996.

Petersen, John. *Reading Women's Stories: Female Characters in the Hebrew Bible*. Minneapolis: Fortress, 2004.

Petersen, Norman R. *Rediscovering Paul: Philemon and the Sociology of Paul's Narrative World*. Minneapolis: Fortress, 1985.

Peterson-Iyer, Karen. "Prostitution: A Feminist Ethical Analysis." In *Journal of Feminist Studies in Religion* 14 (1998) 19–44.

Petitioners for the Abolition of the Slave Trade. *An Abstract of the Evidence Delivered before a Select Committee of the House of Commons in the Years 1790 and 1791 on the Part of the Petitioners for the Abolition of the Slave-Trade*. London, 1791.

Petrie, Glen. *A Singular Iniquity: The Campaigns of Josephine Butler*. New York: Viking, 1971.

Pheterson, Gail, ed. *A Vindication of the Rights of Whores*. Seattle: Seal, 1989.

Phillips, Anthony. "The Laws of Slavery: Exodus 21:2–11." *JSOT* 30 (1984) 51–66.

Phillips, Jerry. "Slave Narratives." In *A Companion to the Literature and Culture of the American South*, edited by Richard Gray and Owen Robinson, 43–57. Oxford: Blackwell, 2004.

Pilch, John J., and Bruce J. Malina, eds. *Handbook of Biblical Social Values*. 2nd ed. Peabody, MA: Hendrickson, 1998.

Pippin, Tina. *Death and Desire: The Rhetoric of Gender in the Apocalypse of John*. Louisville, KY: Westminster John Knox, 1992.

Pisani, Elizabeth. *The Wisdom of Whores: Bureaucrats, Brothels and the Business of AIDS*. London: Granta, 2008.

Pivar, David J. *Purity and Hygiene: Women, Prostitution, and the "American Plan."* Westport, CT: Greenwood, 2002.

———. *Purity Crusade: Sexual Morality and Social Control 1868–1900*. Westport, CT: Greenwood, 1973.

Pleins, David J. *The Social Visions of the Hebrew Bible: A Theological Introduction*. Louisville, KY: Westminster John Knox, 2002.

Pressler, Carolyn. *The View of Women Found in the Deuteronomic Family Laws*. Berlin: de Gruyter, 1993.

Priest, Josiah. *Slavery, as It Relates to the Negro or African Race, Examined in the Light of Circumstances, History and the Holy Scriptures; with an Account of the Origin of the Black Man's Color, Causes of His State of Servitude and traces of His Character as Well in Ancient as in Modern Times: With Strictures on Abolitionism*. Albany, NY: Van Benthuysen, 1843.

Primoratz, Igor. *Ethics and Sex*. London: Routledge, 1999.

Raboteau, Albert J. *Slave Religion: The "Invisible Institution" in the Antebellum South*. 2nd ed. Oxford: Oxford University Press, 2004.

Radner, Ephraim. *Leviticus*. SCM Theological Commentary on the Bible. London: SCM, 2008.

Ramsay, James. *Essay on the Treatment and Conversion of African Slaves in the British Sugar Colonies*. London: Phillips, 1784.

———. *Examination of the Rev Mr Harris's Scriptural Researches on the Licitness of the Slave Trade*. London: Phillips, 1788.

Ranke-Heinemann, Uta. *Eunuchs for the Kingdom of Heaven: The Catholic Church and Sexuality*. Translated by Peter Heinegg. New York: Penguin, 1990.

Reardon, Bernard M. G. *Religious Thought in the Victorian Age: A Survey from Coleridge to Gore*. 2nd ed. London: Longman, 1995.

Reventlow, Henning Graf. *The Authority of the Bible and the Rise of the Modern World*. London: SCM, 1984.

Rice, Madeliene Hooke. *American Catholic Opinion in the Slavery Controversy*. Gloucester, MA: Smith, 1964.

Richards, David A. J. "Commerical Sex and the Rights of the Person: A Moral Argument for the Decriminalization of Prostitution." *University of Pennsylvania Law Review* 127 (1979) 1195–1287.

Richards, Phillip "The Joseph Story as Slave Narrative: On Genesis and Exodus as Prototypes for Early Black Anglophone Writing." In *African Americans and the Bible: Sacred Texts and Social Textures,* edited by Vincent L. Wimbush, 221–35. New York: Continuum, 2000.

Richardson, Alan. "Slavery and Romantic Writers." In *A Companion to Romanticism*, edited by Duncan Wu, 460–69. Oxford: Blackwell, 1998.

Ricoeur, Paul. *The Rule of Metaphor*. London: Routledge, 1978.

————. *The Symbolism of Evil*. Boston: Beacon, 1967.

Ringdal, Nils Johan. *Love for Sale: A World History of Prostitution*. Translated by R. Daly. New York: Grove, 2004.

Ringe, Sharon H. *Jesus, Liberation, and the Biblical Jubilee: Images for Ethics and Christology*. 1985. Reprint. Eugene, OR: Wipf & Stock, 2004.

————. "Jubilee, year of." In *The New Interpreters' Dictionary of the Bible* vol 3, edited by Katharine Doob Sakenfeld, 418–19. Nashville: Abingdon, 2008.

Rollins, Wayne G. "Slavery in the NT." In *The Interpreter's Dictionary of the Bible: An Illustrated Encyclopedia. Supplementary Volume,* edited by Keith Crim, 830–32. Nashville: Abingdon, 1976.

Rosner, Brian S. "Temple Prostitution in 1 Corinthians 6:12–20" *NovT* 40 (1998) 336–51.

Ross, Fred A. *Slavery Ordained of God*. 1857. Reprint. Miami: Mnemosyne, 1969.

Rossiaud, Jacques *Medieval Prostitution*. Translated by Lydia G. Cochrane. Oxford: Blackwell, 1988.

Rossing, Barabra R. *The Choice between Two Cities: Whore, Bride and Empire in the Apocalypse*. Harrisburg, PA: Trinity, 1999.

Rouselle, Aline. *Porneia: On Desire and the Body in Antiquity*. Translated by Felicia Pheasant. Oxford: Blackwell, 1983.

Rowland, Christopher. *The Open Heaven: A Study of Apocalyptic in Judaism and Early Christianity*. Reprint. Eugene, OR: Wipf & Stock, 2002.

Ruether, Rosemary Radford. *New Woman, New Earth: Sexist Ideologies and Human Liberation*. 20th anniversary ed. Boston: Beacon, 1995.

Russell, Bertrand. *Marriage and Morals*. London: Unwin, 1929.

Ruston, Roger. *Human Rights and the Image of God*. London: SCM, 2004.

S., Miss. *Confessions of a Working Girl*. London: Penguin, 2007.

Sabiston, Elizabeth Jean. "Anglo-American Connections: Elizabeth Gaskell, Harriet Beecher Stowe and the 'Iron of Slavery.'" In *The Discourse of Slavery: Aphra Behn to Toni Morrison,* edited by Carl Plasa and Betty J. Ring, 94–117. Routledge: London, 1994.

Saeed, Fouzia. *Taboo! The Hidden Culture of a Red Light Area*. Karachi: Oxford University Press, 2003.

Sahni, Rohini, et al., eds. *Prostitution and Beyond: An Analysis of Sex Work in India.* New Delhi: Sage, 2008.

Saillant, John. "Origins of African American Hermeneutics in Eighteenth-Century Black Opposition to the Slave Trade and Slavery." In *African Americans and the Bible,* edited by Vincent L. Wimbush, 236–50. New York: Continuum, 2000.

Sanders, Teela. *Paying for Pleasure: Men who Buy Sex.* Cullompton, UK: Willan, 2006.

Sanderson, Judith E. "Nahum." In *The Women's Bible Commentary,* edited by Carol Newsom and Sharon H Ringe, 218–21. Louisville, KY: Westminster John Knox, 1998.

Sandford, Jeremy. *Prostitutes: Portraits of People in the Sexploitation Business.* London: Secker & Warburg, 1975.

Sandnes, Karl Olav. *Body and Belly in the Pauline Epistles.* Cambridge: Cambridge University Press, 2002.

———. "Revised Conventions in Early Christian Paraenesis—'Working Good' in 1 Peter as an Example." In *Early Christian Paraenesis in Context,* edited by James Starr et al., 373–404. Berlin: De Gruyter, 2004.

Sanger, William. *History of Prostitution: Its Extent, Causes and Effects throughout the World.* New York: Harper & Brothers, 1858.

Santos, Narry F. *Slave of All: The Paradox of Authority and Servanthood in the Gospel of Mark.* Sheffield, UK: Sheffield Academic Press, 2003.

Schaberg, Jane. *The Resurrection of Mary Magdalene: Legends, Apocrypha and the Christian Testament.* New York: Continuum, 2004.

Schneiders, Sandra M. *The Revelatory Text: Interpreting the New Testament as Sacred Scripture.* 2nd ed. Collegeville, MN: Liturgical, 1999.

Scholl, Lia Claire. *I (Heart) Sex Workers: A Christian Response to People in the Sex Trade.* St. Louise, MI: Chalice, 2012.

Schottroff, Luise. *The Parables of Jesus.* Translated by Linda M. Maloney. Minneapolis: Augsburg Fortress, 2004.

Schrage, Wolfgang. *The Ethics of the New Testament.* Translated by David E. Green. Edinburgh: T. & T. Clark, 1982.

Schulte, H. "Beobachten zum Begriff der Zônâ im Alten Testament." *ZAW* 104 (1992) 255–62.

Scott, George Ryley. *The History of Prostitution.* London: Senate, 1968.

Selman, M. J. "Law." In *Dictionary of the Old Testament: Pentateuch,* edited by David W. Baker and Desmond Alexander, 497–515. Downers Grove, IL: IVP Academic, 2003.

Sewall, Samuel. *The Selling of Joseph: A Memorial.* Boston: Green and Allen, 1700.

Shannon, David T. "An Anti-bellum Sermon: A Resource for an African American Hermeneutic." In *Stony the Road We Trod: African American Biblical Interpretation,* edited by Cain Hope Felder, 98–123. Minneapolis: Fortress, 1991.

Sharp, Carolyn J. *Irony and Meaning in the Hebrew Bible.* Bloomington, IN: Indiana University Press, 2009.

Sharp, Granville. *The Just Limitation on Slavery in the Laws of God: An Essay on Slavery, Proving from Scripture Its Inconsistency with Humanity and Religion.* London: B. White, and E. and C. Dilly, 1776.

———. *Law of Liberty or Royal Law by which All Mankind Will Certainly Be Judged!* London: B. White, and E. and C. Dilly, 1776.

Shaw, Ian. *High Calvinists in Action.* Oxford: Oxford University Press, 2002.

Sheehan, Jonathan. *The Enlightenment Bible: Translation, Scholarship, Culture.* Princeton: Princeton University Press, 2005.

Shelley, Louise. *Human Trafficking: A Global Perspective*. New York: Cambridge University Press, 2010.

Sherwood, Yvonne. *The Prostitute and the Prophet: Hosea's Marriage in Literary-Theoretical Perspective*. Sheffield, UK: Sheffield Academic Press, 1996.

Shields, Mary E. *Circumscribing the Prostitute: The Rhetorics of Intertextuality, Metaphor and Gender in Jeremiah 3:1—4:4*. London: T. & T. Clark, 2004.

Shrage, Laurie. *Moral Dilemmas of Feminism: Prostitution, Adultery, and Abortion*. New York: Routledge, 1994.

Siebert, Eric A. *The Violence of Scripture: Overcoming the Old Testament's Troubling Legacy*. Minneapolis: Fortress, 2012.

Simmons, Melanie. "Theorising Prostitution: The Question of Agency." In *Sex Work and Sex Workers*, edited by Barry M. Dank and Roberto Refinetti, 125–48. Sexuality and Culture Series, vol. 2. New Brunswick: Transaction, 1999.

Skilbrei, May-Len, and Charlotta Holmström. *Prostitution Policy in the Nordic Region: Ambiguous Sympathies*. Farnham, UK: Ashgate, 2013.

Smith, Carol. "Samson and Delilah: A Parable of Power?" *JSOT* 76 (1997) 45–57.

———. "The Story of Tamar: A Power-filled Challenge to the Structures of Power." In *Women in the Biblical Tradition*, edited by George J. Brooke, 16–28. Lampeter, UK: Mellen, 1992.

Smith, Danny. *Slavery Now and Then*. Eastbourne, UK: Kingsway, 2007.

Smith, H. Shelton. *In His Image, But...: Racism in Southern Religion, 1780–1910*. Durham, NC: Duke University Press, 1972.

Smith, Mark M. *Debating Slavery: Economy and Society in the Antebellum American South*. Cambridge: Cambridge University Press, 1998.

Snell, Daniel C. *Flight and Freedom in the Ancient Near East*. Leiden: Brill, 2001.

Soderlund, Jean R. *Quakers and Slavery: A Divided Spirit*. Princeton: Princeton University Press, 1985.

Soh, C. Sarah. *The Comfort Women: Sexual Violence and Postcolonial Memory in Korea and Japan*. Chicago: University of Chicago Press, 2008.

Song, Chan-Seng. "The Black Experience of the Exodus." In *Black Theology: A Documentary History, 1966–1979*, edited by Gayroud S. Wilmore and James H. Cone, 568–83. Maryknoll, NY: Orbis, 1979.

Stead, W. T. *The Maiden Tribute of Modern Babylon: The Report of the Secret Commission*, edited by Antony E. Simpson. Lambertville, NJ: True Bill, 2007.

Sterk, Claire E. *Tricking and Tripping: Prostitution in the era of AIDS*. Putnam Valley, NY: Social Change Press, 1999.

Stott, Anne. *Hannah More: The First Victorian*. Oxford: Oxford University Press, 2003.

Stowe, Harriet Beecher. *Uncle Tom's Cabin*. 1852. Ware, UK: Wordsworth Editions, 1995.

Streete, Gail Corrington. *The Strange Woman: Power and Sex in the Bible*. Louisville, KY: Westminster John Knox, 1997.

Svanstrom, Yvonne. "Prostitution in Sweden: Debates, Practices and Policies 1980–2004." In *International Approaches to Prostitution: Law and Policy in Europe and Asia*, edited by Nicole Westmarland and Geetanjali Gongoli, 67–90. Bristol, UK: Policy, 2006.

Swaminathan, Srividhya. *Debating the Slave Trade: Rhetoric of British National Identity 1759–1815*. Farnham, UK: Ashgate, 2009.

Swanepoel, M. G. "Ezekiel 16: Abandoned Child, Bride Adorned or Unfaithful Wife?" In *Among the Prophets: Language, Image and Structure in the Prophetic Writings*, edited by Philip R. Davies and David J. A. Clines, 84–104. Sheffield, UK: Sheffield Academic Press, 1993.

Teugels, Lieve. "The Anonymous Matchmaker: An Enquiry into the Characterisation of the Servant of Abraham in Genesis 24." *JSOT* 65 (1995) 13–23.

Thistleton, Anthony C. "Canon, Community and Theological Construction." In *Canon and Biblical Interpretation*, edited by Craig Bartholomew et al., 24–27. Grand Rapids: Zondervan, 2006.

————. *The First Epistle to the Corinthians: A Commentary on the Greek Text.* New International Greek Testament Commentary Grand Rapids: Eerdmans, 2000.

Thomas, Helen. *Romanticism and Slave Narratives.* Cambridge: Cambridge University Press, 2000.

Thomas, John L., ed. *Slavery Attacked: The Abolitionist Crusade.* Englewood Cliffs, NJ: Prentice-Hall, 1965.

Thompson, Richard P. "Gathered at the Table: Holiness and Ecclesiology in the Gospel of Luke." In *Holiness and Ecclesiology in the New Testament*, edited by Kent E. Brower and Andy Johnson, 76–94. Grand Rapids: Eerdmans, 2007.

Thompson, Thomas. *The African Trade for Negro Slaves Shewn to be Consistent with Principles of Humanity, and with the Laws of revealed Religion.* Canterbury, 1772.

Tise, Larry A. *Proslavery: A History of the Defense of Slavery in America, 1701–1840.* Athens, GA: University of Georgia Press, 1987.

Tomkins, Stephen. *The Clapham Sect: How Wilberforce's Circle Transformed Britain.* Oxford: Lion Hudson, 2010.

Torbett, David. *Theology and Slavery: Charles Hodge and Horace Bushnell.* Macon, GA: Mercer University Press, 2006.

Truong, Thanh-Dan. *Sex, Money and Morality: Prostitution and Tourism in Southeast Asia.* London: Zed, 1990.

Tucker, Gene M. "The Law in the Eighth Century Prophets." In *Canon, Theology and Old Testament Interpretation: Essays in Honour of B. S. Childs*, edited by Gene M. Tucker et al., 201–16. Philadelphia: Fortress, 1988.

Urbach, E. E. *The Laws Regarding Slavery.* New York: Arno, 1979.

Van Der Toorn, Karel. "Female Prostitution in Payment of Vows in Ancient Israel." *JBL* 108 (1989) 193–205.

Verhey, Allen. *Remembering Jesus: Christian Community, Scripture and the Moral Life.* Grand Rapids: Eerdmans, 2002.

Verner, David C. *The Household of God: The Social World of the Pastoral Epistles.* Chico, CA: Scholars, 1983.

Voltaire. "A Philosophical Dictionary." 1764. In *The Works of Voltaire*, edited by Lord Morley, Vol. VII, 213. New York: Dingwall Rock, 1901. Reprinted in *Slavery: Oxford Readers*, edited by Engerman et al., 24–25. Oxford: Oxford University Press, 2001.

Walkowitz, Judith R. *Prostitution and Victorian Society: Women, Class and the State.* Cambridge: Cambridge University Press, 1980.

Wall, Robert W. "The Significance of a Canonical Perspective of the Church's Scripture." In *The Canon Debate*, edited by Lee Martin McDonald and James A. Sanders, 528–40. Peabody, MA: Hendrickson, 2002.

Waltzer, Michael. *Exodus and Revolution.* New York: Basic, 1985.

Walvin, James. *The Trader, the Owner, the Slave: Parallel Lives in the Age of Slavery.* London: Cape, 2007.

Ward, Benedicta. *Harlots of the Desert: A Study of Repentance in Early Monastic Sources.* London: Mowbray, 1987.

Watts, James W. *Reading Law: The Rhetorical Shaping of the Pentateuch.* Sheffield, UK: Sheffield Academic Press, 1999.

Webb, William J. *Slaves, Women and Homosexuals: Exploring the Hermeneutics of Cultural Analysis.* Downers Grove, IL: IVP, 2001.

Webster, John. *Holy Scripture: A Dogmatic Sketch.* Cambridge: Cambridge University Press, 2003.

Wedd, Mary. "Literature and Religion." In *A Companion to Romanticism,* edited by Duncan Wu, 61–71. Oxford: Blackwell, 1999.

Weems, Renita J. *Battered Love: Marriage, Sex and Violence in the Hebrew Prophets.* Minneapolis: Augsburg Fortress, 1995.

Wegner, Judith Romney. *Chattel or Person? The Status of Women in the Mishnah.* New York: Oxford University Press, 1988.

Weinfeld, Moshe. *Deuteronomy and the Deuteronomic School.* Oxford: Clarendon, 1972.

———. *The Place of the Law in the Religion of Ancient Israel.* Leiden: Brill, 2004.

———. *Social Justice in Ancient Israel and in the Ancient Near East.* Minneapolis: Fortress, 1995.

Weisberg, Dvora E. "The Widow of our Discontent: Levirate Marriage in the Bible and Ancient Israel." *JSOT* 28 (2004) 403–29.

Weissbrodt, David S. *Abolishing Slavery and its Contemporary Forms.* New York: Office of the United Nations High Commissioner for Human Rights, 2002.

Weitzer, Ronald. "The Politics of Prostitution in America." In *Sex for Sale: Prostitution, Pornography and the Sex Industry,* edited by Ronald Weitzer, 159–80. London: Routledge, 2000.

Weld, Theodore D. *Weld's Slavery as It Is: Testimony of a Thousand Witnesses.* New York, 1839.

Wenham, Gordon J. "The Gap between Law and Ethics in the Bible." *JJS* 48 (1997) 17–29.

———. "Why Does Sexual Intercourse Defile? (Lev 15:18)." *ZAW* 95 (1983) 432–34.

Wesley, John. *Thoughts upon Slavery.* London: Hawes, 1774.

Westbrook, Raymond. *Property and the Family in Biblical Law.* JSOTSS 13. Sheffield, UK: Sheffield Academic Press, 1991.

———. "Slave and Master in Ancient Near Eastern Law." *Chicago-Kent Law Review* 70 (1995) 1631–76.

Westermann, William L. *The Slave Systems of Greek and Roman Antiquity.* Philadelphia: The American Philosophical Society, 1955.

Westmarland, Nicole, and Geetanjali Gongoli, eds. *International Approaches to Prostitution: Law and Policy in Europe and Asia.* Bristol: Policy, 2006.

Whitekettle, Richard. "Leviticus 15:18 Reconsidered: Chiasm, Spatial Structure and the Body." *JSOT* 49 (1991) 31–45.

Whyte, Iain. *Scotland and the Abolition of Black Slavery 1756–1838.* Edinburgh: Edinburgh University Press, 2006.

Wiedemann, T. E. J. *Slavery.* New Surveys in the Classics No 19. Oxford: Clarendon, 1987.

Wilberforce, William. *A Practical View of the Prevailing Religious System of Professed Christians.* 1797. Reprint. London, 1829.

Williams, Roger. "Beyond Wolfenden? Prostitution. Politics and the Law." 1986. Reprinted in *Prostitution,* edited by Roger Matthews and Maggie O' Neill, 491–513. Farnham, UK: Ashgate, 2003.

Wilson, A. "The Pragmatics of Politeness and Pauline Epistolography: A Case Study of the Letter to Philemon." *JSNT* 48 (1992) 107–19.

Wimbush Vincent L. "The Bible and African Americans: An Outline of an Interpretive History." In *Stony the Road We Trod: African American Biblical Interpretation*, edited by Cain Hope Felder, 81–97. Minneapolis: Fortress, 1991.

Winter, Bruce W. *After Paul Left Corinth: The Influence of Secular Ethics and Social Change*. Grand Rapids: Eerdmans, 2001.

Winter, S. C. "Paul's Letter to Philemon." *NTS* 33 (1987) 1–15.

Wolff, Hans W. *Joel and Amos: A Commentary on the Books of the Prophets Joel and Amos*. Philadelphia: Fortress, 1977.

Wolffe, John. *The Expansion of Evangelicalism: The Age of Wilberforce, More, Chalmers and Finley*. Nottingham, UK: IVP, 2006.

Wood, Marcus. *The Poetry of Slavery: An Anglo-American Anthology 1764–1865*. Oxford: Oxford University Press, 2003.

Woolman, John. *Some Considerations on the Keeping of Negroes, Recommended to the Professors of Christianity of Every Denomination*. Philadelphia: Gehenna, 1754.

Wright, Christopher J. H. "Jubilee, Year of." *Anchor Bible Dictionary*, 1025–30. New York: Doubleday, 1992.

———. *Old Testament Ethics for the People of God*. Leicester, UK: IVP, 2004.

———. "Response to Gordon McConville." In *Canon and Biblical Interpretation*, edited by Craig G. Bartholomew et al., 282–90. Scripture and Hermeneutics, vol. 7. Milton Keynes, UK: Paternoster, 2006.

Wright, N. T. *Scripture and the Authority of God*. London: SPCK, 2005.

Wright, Stephen I. *The Voice of Jesus: Studies in the Interpretation of Six Gospel Parables*. Carlisle, UK: Paternoster, 2000.

Wu, Rose. "Women on the Boundary: Prostitution, Contemporary and in the Bible." *Feminist Theology* 28 (2001) 69–81.

Young, Franklin, W. "The Relation of Clement to the Epistle of James." *JBL* 67 (1948) 339–45.

Zelnick-Abramovitz, R. *Not Wholly Free: The Concept of Manumission and the Status of Manumitted Slaves in the Ancient Greek World*. Leiden: Brill, 2005.

Zenger, Erich. "The God of Exodus in the Message of the Prophets as Seen in Isaiah." In *Exodus A Lasting Paradigm*, edited by Bas van Iersel & Anton Weiler, 22–33. Concilium 189. Edinburgh: T. & T. Clark, 1987.

Zimmerli, Walther. *Ezekiel 1: A Commentary on the Book of the Prophet Ezekiel, Chapters 1–24*. Translated by Ronald E. Clements. Minneapolis: Fortress, 1979.

Zimmermann, Yvonne C. *Other Dreams of Freedom: Religion, Sex and Human Trafficking*. New York: Oxford University Press, 2013.